Not Another Book for New Teachers:

12 tips to guide you through your first year of Primary Teaching

ABERMORE PUBLISHING

Survival Tips for New Teachers: 12 tips to guide you through your first year of Primary Teaching

Copyright © 2022 Mark Watson.

All rights reserved. This book or any portion thereof may not be reproduced or used in any manner whatsoever without the express written permission of the publisher except for the use of brief quotations in a book review.

First printing, 2022.

Abermore Publishing, an imprint of Aberlochaber Publishing Ltd.

Aberdeen, Scotland

www.facebook.com/MarkWatsonAuthor

www.instagram.com/MarkWatsonAuthor

ABERMORE PUBLISHING

ABERLOCHABER PUBLISHING

Contents

Introduction – Who are You? Who am I? – Page 1

Tip # 1 – Where to Start – Page 4

Tip # 2 – You Should Probably Sort Your Class Out – Page 21

Tip # 3 – Build Up Those Relationships – Page 40

Tip # 4 – Get the Learning Right – Page 47

Tip # 5 – Keep Your Class Safe – Page 59

Tip # 6 – What is Expected of You – Page 72

Tip # 7 – You're a Professional, Act Like It – Page 81

Tip # 8 – Parental Guidance – Page 87

Tip # 9 – Find a Friend – Page 95

Tip # 10 – Continual Professional Development – Page 100

Tip # 11 – Get a Life – Page 108

Tip # 12 – Expect the Unexpected – Page 113get

A Final Word – Page 119

References – Page 120

Index – Page 128

To my wife, who continues to put up with every ridiculous idea or plan that I come up with and helps me to see it through.

Introduction

Who Am I?

Who Are You?

Hello, I am a teacher. I have taught for several years, primarily within the Primary School setting. In those years I have had lots of ups and **several** downs. I have had moments where I've considered myself to be the greatest teacher in the land, and moments where I questioned whether I should be in the profession at all. In the beginning, I hit rock bottom in my teaching career when I effectively failed my NQT year (I'll explain why later) but since then, I've had many highs such as becoming the Assistant Head Teacher in an International School for children aged 3 - 16, with my main responsibility being for the Early Years and Primary School within that. Professionally, I have also tutored within a university on courses for teachers in training and nursery practitioners working towards a degree. But realistically, the above means nothing to you – and why should it? This book isn't about what I am or have been. It's about **you**.

So, who are you? This really is the key question that you should be asking yourself now. You've passed your last exams; you've written that final essay; you've been given that final score, that final grade which decides what 'level' of degree you will be getting. But after all that hard work at college/university in teacher-training, the question still remains: **Who are you**?

This is a question I asked many students who were getting ready to graduate when I was asked to be a 'Guest Lecturer'. Although I often received a variety of answers, the most common answer I was given was that they were now a "teacher". Which begged the question: what on earth have you been for the past few months of teacher training? What has changed so much in those last few months that has now made you a 'teacher' and no longer a 'student-teacher'? A piece of paper? A symbolic or numerical grade? If you are basing the fact that you are now a teacher solely on the documentation of a 'degree', think again. Presuming you have successfully passed your degree, you were a teacher **way** before that – so give yourself some credit because you're right – you *are* a teacher. But what does that actually mean?

You are about to embark on a new life, a new vocation, something that will consume every ounce of energy you have. It will bring you tears of sadness and it will give you tears of joy. You will have an entire spectrum of emotions in just the first few months of your new career, never mind the rest that is to come.

Inspired by the experiences of colleagues and myself in roles as class teachers or Senior Leadership, I've generated 12 tips to help you survive your first year out of university in a classroom of your own. Each overarching 'tip' has several sub-sections designed to target all of your needs and questions. This book is intended to be as frank as possible; to tell you how it is; to actually give you advice and help you avoid that sinking feeling. It will be blunt, but it will be honest. I sincerely hope that these tips will help you through your first year in teaching and every year after.

In this book, I will refer to some educational theories and reference other authors work, all of which will be cited at the end. There are so many excellent people with advice out there, it would be a shame to miss them out. Good luck!

Tip #1
Where to Start

Who You Are

I asked in the introduction: 'Who are you?' Hopefully, you managed to think of an answer which pertained to both your personality and your professionality.

Now, who would **I** say that you are?

You are now a <u>respected</u> member of a community – remember that! You're about to become a part of a small area, be it in a leafy suburb; a deprived urban setting or an isolated country setting (the number of different settings is endless). Nonetheless, you are now a key part of that community, a person that children and parents will stop to say 'hello' to. A person who is now a celebrity to many children who see you outside the school setting. You will be held to high expectations and standards in your personal life as well as your professional life.

As such, you are also now a professional. A person in charge of the lives of up to thirty-three children and possibly the leader of a small team (pupil support assistant, support for learning, etc). You might be just out of university, in your early twenties and are now expected to direct members of staff who are twice your age and have been in their job since before you were born! You are now expected to lead these children and adults to a year of success.

But let's get practical – where do you start when you finally receive that message telling you which school you are going to teach in for your first year?

Community

Many of you will have been instructed, during teacher training, to conduct some form of 'community walk'. I also know that many of you **probably** didn't do this walk or probably didn't do it with enough criticality. But why is this so important? As previously mentioned, you are now a part of this community. You need to have a good understanding of this community to support your children, parents and school. You need to know what is available within your local area. Are there play parks; green spaces; shops; local community projects; sports clubs; libraries? What can these spaces or amenities mean for both your teaching this year and what do they mean in the world of your children?

To many of the children that you teach, they may not have ventured far from their local area, meaning that the large supermarket down the road from the school could be a key part of their world. Whereas you may be in an area where the children's world expands far and wide, giving you ample areas to access and use to interact with your class.

You also must consider the socio-economics of your school's local area. Are the children in this area from families who are very affluent; families who rely on social benefits; families who do not have English as their first language? All of these factors can greatly affect how you plan the rest of your year with your class but also with the rest of the school community. Knowing where you are going to be working can make a difference to the experience your class have for the next year and for every year to come. So, spend time learning about **where** you are going to be teaching. It doesn't have to be a physical community walk like many of you were expected to do in your teacher training. But go for a drive, go to a local café, speak to the local staff. Find out where you are – as if it's anything like where I taught for several years, it can feel like a completely different world.

Classroom Setup – Furniture & Layout

So, you've finally figured out where your school is and arrived at the front door. You've said your nervous "Hello" to the member of the Senior Leadership Team (otherwise referred to as the 'Senior Management Team, Head Teacher, Depute/Assistant Head Teacher; Principal or Principal Teacher) and then they take you through to your very first classroom and leave you to your thoughts. Finally, everything you've been working towards has led to this moment. Your heart beats faster, excited but nervous at what is about to come. This is it. Your class. Your legacy.

Then you stand there. Mind blank or mind whizzing, "What on earth do I do now?" Every amazing idea you've ever had before has now left your brain and you're stood facing a load of unorganised tables, chairs and cabinets with pieces of odd coloured paper hanging loosely from staples on the wall. There's probably a couple of random pieces of stationery lying around and, perhaps, even some textbooks. This begs the question, which this chapter aims to address: Where to start?

First things first, before you even enter your classroom look for inspiration from various sources: consider examples you have seen from your student experience; look at teaching pages on social media; pop your head into other classrooms within the school you are now in; install the Pinterest app and get lost in the many fabulous ideas, but stay realistic not all school classrooms, budgets or resources will allow you to create the 'Perfect Pinterest Palace'. Remember you are creating a place for learning, not entering *'Grand Designs'*.

Now, grab a piece of paper and draw a rough sketch of how you think your class could look. It's not meant to be a work of art, just a simple idea of how your classroom might look when it's all pieced together. Consider the following things:

- How many children will you have in your class – therefore how many tables and chairs will you need? Do you have enough?
- Do you have other furniture that you need to have – cabinets or shelves that can be moved? Do you have enough?
- If you are teaching younger children, you may need to have some role play; arts & crafts or play areas for the children. Is there furniture for this? Do you need to get some?

When you've considered these things and have drawn a rough plan for your classroom, spend some time moving things roughly into place (you may want to get somebody in to help you unless you've been hitting the gym recently. Tables and cabinets are surprisingly heavy). Some teachers prefer just to get stuck in and start moving furniture around until it looks like they want it to look. If that system works, fair enough but I would always advise having an idea of **what** you want it to look like – especially if it's your first year.

For me, this part is very important - once you have planned your room on paper have a walk through it as though your children were actually there. Sit or stand where you would be when teaching your lesson, can you see everyone? Where are your children when you're teaching – on the carpet, in their chairs, do they have the freedom of movement? Where are their resources – can they easily access any materials they need, will the setup cause a bottleneck and disruption to your class? **Is there anything which is clearly unsafe?** Have a walk through and make any changes that you think will help but remember: this is **your** classroom, you can make changes any time you want to or need to. If something isn't working, don't let it continue for days on end, **change it.**

I will say, and this is vitally important, so I will reiterate throughout the book, that you must **SPEAK** to colleagues and management. Find out if there are any compulsory setup arrangements or expectations. This could include things such as a reading corner in your room or a 'break-out' space for children who need time to calm down. While you may have to conform to some compulsory expectations set by your Senior Leadership Team, remember – this is your class, it has to work for you and your style. If it's not your style and doesn't work for you, I promise that you will struggle this year. Don't try to be another teacher – be yourself.

Classroom Setup - Walls, Displays & Labels

Walls. It's amazing the differences you can see, and probably have already seen in your experience, on teachers' classroom walls. Some teachers have meticulously arranged displays with perfect borders where it appears (and in some cases, probably have) they used a spirit level to ensure accuracy; and colour-coded schemes which are relevant to today's interior design styles; whereas others have done the bare minimum, just getting things up on a wall to avoid having Senior Leadership Team getting upset at them.

So, what do you need to have on your walls? There's a range of things you could have on your walls but the key things I think you'll want to have is: an area to display children's learning; an area to display supporting resources (such as VCOP displays or multiplication tables); a behaviour management chart; and possibly a learning journey? This all comes down to what your school expects. I've taught in schools where there was complete freedom; one where I needed to have one wall dedicated to Maths, Literacy, and Health & Wellbeing; I've taught in a school where they were more focused on Learning Journeys, inspired by John Hattie's 'Visible Learning' (2008; 2012), and wasn't interested in displaying the children's work. There are a million ideas of what you can do to your walls in your class but use them effectively to help your class.

Displays themselves are always a contentious issue (Chesebrough and King, 2004; Katz, Chard and Kogan, 2014) as to whether they should be bright and engaging with lots of things or whether they should be simple to avoid distracting students or being overstimulating for children with additional support needs. With regards to this, it depends greatly on the children in your class (you can learn either from handover notes or once you get to know your class – remember you can change things). Which leads us onto whether you will actually spend time changing your displays. Many would argue that you should be changing your displays regularly to keep them relevant. Many teachers, like myself at times, forget to keep up with changing them. It's a simple and common mistake – you have hundreds of things to keep on top of never mind making sure your displays you constantly changing. This is why I recently adopted the use of a large learning journey display (See Figure 1) as it was a year-long process and meant that the display could stay up all year without having to be changed. Make sure that your displays are worthwhile, useful and not causing you too much stress or anguish. Trust me, you will have enough on your plate as it is without worrying whether you changed a spelling display or not. Quite often, the most effective method of using wall displays is in collaboration with the students, meaning you put things up on the wall with the children as they learn. To some extent, this gives you more time to create effective wall displays over the year and allows the children to feel proud of their input in decorating their classroom (Hargreaves and Fullan, 2012).

Labels are something that most classrooms have, partially for peace of mind and partially for ownership. As teachers, we often label children's trays or coat peg. We label resources so that we can train children to know where to go when they need something. Something else to consider, especially given the rise in numbers – there were 30,000+ EAL children in Scotland in 2018 (Scottish Government, 2019), is to consider having labels to help support and assimilate your children who are not yet fluent in English. Consider having labels in relevant foreign languages and English to help children. Furthermore, having labels on various things in your classroom can help to create a literacy-rich environment. This helps to immerse your students in English by helping them learn to read and say context-based phrases (Coelho, 2012; Dodd, 2017).

Figure 1 – Example of Learning Journey Display

Classroom Setup – Get to know your resources

Resources. Every school has different resources, partially to meet different needs but also because previous teachers have liked or disliked other resources which have then been removed or thrown out. Often, most new teachers I've spoken to, struggle to come to terms with the school not having this 'amazing resource that we had at my last school'. I think if you've been teaching for more than 3 years, you've heard that phrase at least 20 times. We get it, there is probably a better resource that you have seen before but this is what you have. School budgets are often tighter than you'd imagine and are not always able to spend a large sum of money on a new resource. Particularly not on the advice of a new teacher – that's no disrespect to you, I'd be willing to bet that the resource you're pitching is fantastic, but Senior Leadership will not spend a large amount of money on somebody they don't fully know or trust yet.

So, you're stuck with the resources in your school. Have a look at what there is, rake around in the older boxes (sometimes there are a few excellent 'ancient resources') or see what is already in your classroom. Find what there is and decide what you are going to use to teach with. Remember, you can change your resources throughout the year if they aren't working, but find a place to start.

Once you've found the resources that you are going to use to teach your class, get to know them (hence the sub-title) as you must know where you can go with this resource to support your children's learning. Are there multiple resources you can use in tandem? I can recall one maths scheme being great for giving arithmetic practise on pages, where there were more than fifty adding and subtraction questions for children to practise; whereas I used another maths scheme to support the use of problem-solving, as the other one available wasn't as effective. You'll learn through time which resources to go to but remember to ask more experienced teachers within the school. If you have a stage partner (a colleague in your school who teaches the same age group), see what they've used or check with whoever taught your stage last year. Additionally, check what concrete resources you have for teaching. Many schools have bought into various resources over the years to encourage teachers into more active and hands-on learning. Check the resources room in your school, they might have the latest concrete resource that many schools have bought into, but there is often another resource hidden at the back of a cupboard that nobody is using which might work perfectly for you.

Lastly, and most importantly, get to know your curriculum. In the UK, there are different curriculums. Having taught using two of these curriculums, they are mostly the same content but fashioned differently. These curriculums are your lifeline. They are what you need to follow to ensure you are meeting the governmental and curricular expectations of teaching and learning. Most curriculums are a progression of learning and show where the learner is going next in that area of learning (e.g. they have learned to add 10 to a number mentally, now you should teach them to add multiples of 10 to a number mentally). The main difference that you will find with curriculums is how they are to be administered. Some curriculums, such as the Scottish Curriculum for Excellence (Scottish Executive, 2004, Figure 2), are broader and more generalised, meaning that learners in your class are working within a level for several years before they've achieved their expected target; whereas some are more specific, such as The English National Curriculum (Department for Education, 2013, Figures 3 & 4), meaning they have set goals that are expected to be achieved by each learner by the end of each year. There are definitely both pros and cons to the structure of each of these systems, but the main thing is that you follow their direction.

Remember – you do not follow a textbook, resource or a scheme of work. You follow a child's learning and the curriculum. The textbook, resource or scheme of work are tools for you to teach, they do not tell you what to teach.

Number, money and measure			
	Early	First	Second
Number and number processes including addition, subtraction, multiplication, division and negative numbers	I have explored numbers, understanding that they represent quantities, and I can use them to count, create sequences and describe order. *MNU 0-02a* I use practical materials and can 'count on and back' to help me to understand addition and subtraction, recording my ideas and solutions in different ways. *MNU 0-03a*	I have investigated how whole numbers are constructed, can understand the importance of zero within the system and can use my knowledge to explain the link between a digit, its place and its value. *MNU 1-02a* I can use addition, subtraction, multiplication and division when solving problems, making best use of the mental strategies and written skills I have developed. *MNU 1-03a*	I have extended the range of whole numbers I can work with and having explored how decimal fractions are constructed, can explain the link between a digit, its place and its value. *MNU 2-02a* Having determined which calculations are needed, I can solve problems involving whole numbers using a range of methods, sharing my approaches and solutions with others. *MNU 2-03a*

Figure 2 – A Curriculum for Excellence: Outcomes for Early Level to Fourth Level – Number and Number Processes

Year 1 programme of study

Number – number and place value

Statutory requirements

Pupils should be taught to:

- count to and across 100, forwards and backwards, beginning with 0 or 1, or from any given number
- count, read and write numbers to 100 in numerals; count in multiples of twos, fives and tens
- given a number, identify one more and one less
- identify and represent numbers using objects and pictorial representations including the number line, and use the language of: equal to, more than, less than (fewer), most, least
- read and write numbers from 1 to 20 in numerals and words.

Figure 3 – English National Curriculum: Year 1 Expectations for Number and Place Value

Year 2 programme of study

Number – number and place value

Statutory requirements

Pupils should be taught to:

- count in steps of 2, 3, and 5 from 0, and in tens from any number, forward and backward
- recognise the place value of each digit in a two-digit number (tens, ones)
- identify, represent and estimate numbers using different representations, including the number line
- compare and order numbers from 0 up to 100; use <, > and = signs
- read and write numbers to at least 100 in numerals and in words
- use place value and number facts to solve problems.

Figure 4 – English National Curriculum: Year 2 Expectations for Number and Place Value

CLASSROOM SETUP - SCHOOL SYSTEMS

School systems. How the school runs. How it operates. The school you have been assigned for your first year of teaching will probably operate slightly differently from the last one you were at in teacher training. First, accept that the system of your new school will feel strange at first and you will, undoubtedly, feel that it is inferior to the one you got used to before. Once you get past that feeling, then it is time to get learning how your school works.

Find out how they take registration in the morning, this is vital as it helps to ensure your class are safe and protected, and also helps you avoid upsetting the school administrator or secretary.

How to request maintenance for your physical classroom or your ICT resources. Do you have to fill out a form? Do you need to find a time when maintenance or the janitor is free? Do you need to find that one member of staff who is a computer wizard? Is there an ICT hotline? If there is, add it to your speed-dial.

How does the school manage its lunch system? Do you have to send a child physically to the canteen with lunch numbers and orders? Do they do it online? Do the children all receive a coloured band so that they cannot change their choice of lunch? Do the children still need to use a 'dinner ticket' or is it all online payments now? Find out the method for your school. But also find out, what happens when (inevitably) a child forgets their packed lunch – can you phone home, do they have to get a school lunch or are there other sanctions in place to support this? Also, does your school have a kitchen? Many school lunches are ordered, cooked and prepared at another school and brought in. You must know how these systems work and how they impact upon your children.

Child protection – this is a very important system to get to know. With many of the above systems, you'll learn as you go and probably make mistakes with how they are conducted. With 'Child Protection,' however, there cannot be any mistakes. Every child that walks through the front door of the school is under your care, not just the children in your class. Often during your first in-service/inset days, you will have a presentation about child protection and what the systems are within your school and the local area. Make sure you know what these are and if you are unsure, **ask.** Ensuring you know who to speak to, what to do or record can make the difference between a child remaining in a harmful situation or being protected from it.

WHO ARE THE MOST IMPORTANT PEOPLE IN THE SCHOOL?

This is my favourite question to ask student teachers whenever I have been a guest lecturer at a university. Often the first answer I hear is: "The children". To which I laugh and say, "Definitely not!" This answer is, of course, said in tongue and cheek but there is an element of truth to it. There are people who make a school successful other than just teachers and children. Who then are the most important people? What answer am I wanting the students to come to? Many have already made an appearance in this chapter:

- Janitors//Caretaker/Maintenance
- Cleaners

- Cooks and Lunchtime Staff
- Admin Staff
- Teaching Assistants (TA; LA; PSA)
- School Crossing Patrol

These groups are the engine of a school, they keep it running so that you can do your job. Because these groups of people are the 'most important' people in the school, make sure you are kind to them, helpful to them and most importantly – friendly. Without intending to patronise you as a professional, a simple 'please' and 'thank you' goes a long way.

I think of one janitor/caretaker that was in a school I worked in. I spoke to this janitor whenever they walked by and made time to actually converse with them. They later told me that not many teachers actually took the time to treat them as a person and often just barked requests at them. This also led me to learn that, while this janitor was a professional and did all the jobs expected of him, that any request I had for maintenance was usually fast-tracked ahead of anybody else's.

You will need these groups to support you. Apologise sincerely when you are late completing the register or lunch order, explain to the cleaner that you have used glitter today and you will clean up the mess – not them and make a point of conversing with everyone and showing an interest in them. Be friendly.

In your career, you may meet administrators, janitors, cleaners or any member of staff who you find it difficult to connect with, but take the time to work with them and I promise you that it will be worth your while.

Plan of Action

Your first week at school with your first class will fly by so fast, you'll almost miss it. You may not even recall it clearly in ten years' time, but what you will probably recall is the amount of planning you are about to put into this first week.

When you plan your first week, you will still be getting to grips with all of the resources in your new school and all of their routines – so keep things simple. **Ask** the staff in your school or your mentor and check to see if there is anything in particular that you are supposed to do in the first week (Rights Respecting Schools; a particular theme or topic; begin a class novel; create a video introducing your class – the possibilities are limitless) and double-check what the expectations are for how much time should be dedicated to each subject within your timetable. Once you've figured out what is compulsory, start to plan your week. Fill in a simple timetable for the first week (you'll create a proper one later) where you plan when you are going to devote time to teach the classroom management plan; when you will do 'meet & greet' lessons; when you will do assessments. Having these planned out will give you a sense of security in your first week. In your second week, make it similar, with time devoted to practising your classroom management plan, but as you will have some data from baseline assessments, you can begin teaching them content.

SUMMARY OF KEY POINTS

- Check where your school is; figure out what the community is like and check what is available nearby or accessible to the school/children.
- Figure out how you want your classroom to be set out and check for any school expectations of the layout.
- Make your wall displays appealing but manageable. Consider what you may need on your wall and, again, consult your school to see what is required.
- Check what resources you have in the school and decide what you are going to use and how you are going to use them. Make sure to check to see if there are any particular resources that you 'have' to use. (While I disagree with this notion personally, some schools have spent thousands of pounds on resources that they want a return on).
- Learn the school systems quickly to help you assimilate into the school. It will make you feel at home quicker and will stop you from upsetting anybody. Remember, this is more to help you than anybody else.
- Be kind and friendly to non-teaching staff in the school. Even if you are slightly more introverted, try to converse with the non-teaching staff regularly (even just a short "How's your day been?" – Let them have a rant, smile, and move on).
- Keep the plan for your first week simple and concise to settle yourself, before trying to show what you can do in teaching.

Tip #2

You Should Probably Sort Your Class Out

First Day

D-Day. It's your first day on your own in **your** class. You've set your class up, you've organised your tables, you've made your displays and you've met your Teaching Assistant. Now, you're awaiting that bell to ring (or whatever signal there is for your school – believe me, I've seen/heard some *peculiar* ones) to meet these children for the first time (I realise some of you may have briefly met the class before the Summer, but trust me, it's not quite the same).

The bell rings. Your heart stops. You suddenly feel sick. And then you go out to meet them – children of all shapes and sizes and children with a wide range of personalities that you are now responsible for. Compose yourself – they're just children, right?

Okay, **Step 1** – say hello, smile, look excited to see them (even if you are terrified on the inside). Then, get them to line up as best as you can. This will be a different experience for you depending on what age of class you are teaching. For children starting school for the first time, this might be a stressful moment (particularly with the watchful eyes of parents lingering nearby), but please persevere. For older children, ages 7 and up, I would be expecting them to line up properly when you arrive for the first time but this can be practised. When it comes to practising this, make sure they are shown to line up to a high standard (and I mean a **high standard**), be firm with them and, tell or show, them how to get into line properly. Remember, you are now their teacher; you are now the boss - so, act like it. Getting the children to know from the beginning that this is what they do when they arrive at school is vital for your management of them. Don't ask them nicely at this stage – <u>**tell**</u> them: "Line up correctly." Do not bring your class in until they are lined up exactly as they should be. Plevin (2016) explains that you should avoid asking questions, such as "Will you line up?" or "Would you all like to line up now?" You are not offering them a choice in this matter – you are telling them to line up. For me, they are standing in a single file, facing me, in complete silence. Set your standard from the beginning and maintain this standard for the rest of the year – <u>never</u> drop this standard.

Okay – great start, you've got them lined up; they've followed you in inside, and you haven't lost anybody. **Step 2**, tell them how you want them to start their day. Literally. Show and tell them where to hang their jackets/coats; where to hang their P.E./swimming bags; if needed, where they change into indoor shoes; and **how** they enter your classroom. Below (figures 5 & 6) are some examples of my morning routines for when I taught Early Years and 2nd Level/Key Stage 2. You'll notice that the routine is very similar. The only difference was how I approached these – the younger children received a much gentler approach, as often they had no school experience and didn't know what things were or how to do them; the older children were dealt with more firmly, the expectations for them are higher because they have been in school longer (though please note, that does not mean that they will definitely know what to do).

Morning Routine for Primary 1/Reception
1.) Instruct the class to line up – single file is my preference.
2.) Guide class into school.
3.) Children independently hang up jackets and bags.
4.) Children put snack into their tray.
5.) Children sit on their designated spot on the carpet with the teacher.

Figure 5 – Morning Routine for Early Years

Morning Routine for Primary 5-7/Year 4-6
1.) Instruct the class to line up – single file and silent.
2.) Direct class into school.
3.) Children independently hang up jackets, bags and P.E. Kits.
4.) Children hand in any homework or letters to the class teacher.
5.) Children put a snack or their lunchboxes away in the designated area.
6.) Children sit silently and follow morning 'Starter task' (e.g. reading, maths problem or short expressive activity).

Figure 6 – Morning Routine for 2nd Level/Key Stage 2

Okay, Steps 1 & 2 are complete. **Step 3**, classroom management. This is how you expect your class to run. Explain to them how they are to get your attention: do they put their hand up; thumbs up; or shout out? What works for you? How do they go to the toilet: do they just go when they need; do they come and ask you and then go; do you have a toilet pass? What works for you? When they are completing tasks, is there a volume chart; is there a voices chart; does noise simply not bother you? What works for you? It's important to note that there are multiple routines or methods for bringing your class into school. For example, in my morning routine for Primary 1/Reception, I could alter it to have a 'soft-start' for the children rather than have them sit on the carpet.

You'll notice that I repeated a phrase: What works for you? The reason for this is that while most schools want consistency in their approach to classrooms (which I fully understand), it has to be something that you can manage and maintain to be effective within your classroom. For me, I would always tell children to put their hand up to answer a question or tell me something, but would sometimes tell them to shout out answers if they knew them. For children going to the toilet, I always forgot who had asked me which led to two problems – too many out at the toilet together and a fire hazard because I couldn't remember which children were where. My solution was using the toilet pass, children had to put the toilet pass on their desk so that I knew who was where (I even had one for the water fountain). For older students, another option I used was an old lined notebook where the students had to write the time they left the classroom and then write the time they returned to the classroom. This was a very useful method as it allowed students to practise reading the time on a regular basis. For noise, I personally cannot stand silence. I needed some form of background noise in my classroom or it drove me mad, which is probably why I prefer teaching the Early Years and First Level/KS1. But figure out what works for you and command it. I recall an excellent teacher who could not stand noise during tasks unless it was required. He trained his class perfectly so that when he set a task, he didn't need to shout at them to be quiet, they were already quiet and working.

Step 4 – actually get to know them. You are an alien to these children. They don't know you and you don't know them, no matter how many 'hand-over' notes you've read or conversations you've had with prior teachers. You need to learn who they are, what they like and dislike and, arguably most importantly, what makes them 'tick' – how can you get the best out of them? Introduce yourself, this sounds silly but actually tell them how to pronounce your name – especially if you have a 'difficult' name to pronounce. To get around this, I know of a teacher who used '*Miss [First Name]*' because children found her surname too difficult. The respect is still there by using 'Miss', and she checked that this was okay with her Senior Leadership Team, but she made it work for her.

Begin to build relationships with the children in your class. There are numerous activities that are traditionally done to find out more about students (posters, family shield pictures and drawing) but there are also interactive options you could use. Dunn (2017) suggests numerous activities and spins on traditional games to help you get to know your students in a fun and active way, such as "Guess Who" or "Link It" (I highly recommend "Link It"). The activities that you do to get to know your children will vary depending on their age but use your first morning together to set the boundaries and get to know each other. Maths, spelling, writing, reading and everything else can come later. **Behavioural expectations are more important.**

Without these expectations, learning and teaching will be extremely difficult.

Practise Your Routines

Practise. This step is the most vital step in your entire teaching career. Practise your classroom management. Practise your children lining up properly. If they don't do it properly, start over until they do it properly. I recall my first year of teaching when I did this, I practised this for the first week and then forgot about it. This was my first big mistake in teaching – it meant that for the rest of the year, I'd spend precious minutes reminding my class of what they were to do and becoming frustrated when they didn't do it.

When you first get these children into the class, this is your chance to show the children what you expect. Countless authors have said the same thing you must **explain** what the routine is; you must **model** the routine, physically showing them how to do it; then you must get them to **practise** it a few times in front of your eyes to see that they can do it correctly (Cohen, Manion and Morrison, 2004; McEwan, 2006; Rose and Howley, 2007; Reinke, Herman and Sprick, 2011; Chaplain, 2015; Plevin, 2016). This is, similar to the lining up procedure, where you must be critical. If there's something slightly off, get them to redo it until it's perfect. You'd be amazed at how many children do not tuck their chair in properly when they stand up to go somewhere. Show them what to do and how to do it.

You have to practise these routines regularly and after the first few months return to practice if the children begin to forget the expectations, to ensure that the children do these routines without having to think (Plevin, 2017). When I taught Primary 1/Reception, I spent time every day marching them up and down the corridors of the school until they were able to do it perfectly. This got to the point where I could send my class, by themselves, from one end of the school to the other and they would stay in a single file line and not speak. This took practise and resilience to achieve but was worth it in the long run.

Behaviour Management

If only the children all did exactly as they were told, our jobs would be a thousand times easier. Naturally, they don't always do what they are meant to. Therefore, we have to know how to control them. Every classroom that I have walked into has a slightly different management style. Some schools try to have a consistent approach throughout, and while you will have to follow much of this, I would always argue that you may have to adapt it slightly within your classroom to make it work for you. In terms of your approach, there is my preferred method of being an 'unbiased referee' (Linsin, 2013); using positive behaviour management, (Williams, 2017; 2018), or how a good friend of mine explained his management method: *"I'm big, scary and Irish. They just have to do exactly as I say."* (I should note that while this teacher was very strict and firm with how the children behaved, the children all enjoyed being in his class. He was funny and jovial with them, but they all knew where the line was drawn and when to stop misbehaving or being silly).

Now, this isn't a behaviour management book, there are plenty out there which are great examples to use if it is an area you need to work on, such as Bill Rogers, Michael Linsin or Rob Plevin. But I feel it is important to cover a few basics on how to set up your behaviour management system. Much of what I will suggest is inspired from their books, "Dream Class," (2009); "The Classroom Management Secret," (2013); "Classroom Management for Art, Music and PE Teachers" (2014); "Taking Control of the Noisy Class: From Chaos to Calm in 15 Seconds" (2016); "Classroom Management Success In 7 Days or Less" (2017).

First and foremost, I should confess – in my first year of teaching, my behaviour and classroom management was horrendous. There was no control and not enough respect. I can even vividly recall the moment it clicked that I had completely lost control and couldn't hide it any longer. A child in the class was talking over me while I was teaching and I asked (sarcastically) if I was interrupting their conversation. They replied, "Yes." It was then, I knew I was in trouble and questioned whether I could do this job at all. I scraped through the rest of the year and had to do an 'extension' to become a fully qualified teacher.

This, as you can imagine, hit me very hard and I knew I had to do something about it. As I said before, there are many authors who you can go to for advice to help you with behaviour management. For me, I went to Michael Linsin's (2013) "The Classroom Management Secret," and I would not be exaggerating if I said that his words saved my career. The way he mapped out behaviour and classroom management made perfect sense to me and it was something I knew that I could apply effectively to my classroom. In recent years, I have read widely of Rob Plevin to supplement my learning and enhance my practice.

How your behaviour management plan works will depend principally upon how the overarching school behaviour plan works. You must check what consequences the school allows and whether you are allowed to add to them within your class setting. Where possible, avoid 'upsetting the apple cart' by not sticking to a consistent approach within the school but remember that this behaviour management system has to work for you. What you can affect is the rules/expectations within your classroom. I recall at university and through some readings (Knoester, 2012; Miller, 2016), that class rules should be created in collaboration with children as it helps for them to create ownership of the rules – the idea being that if they break them, they're breaking their own rules. In my experience, I've found that most children aren't too upset about that. Therefore, I would advocate that a teacher sets their own rules and explains them to the class. This allows you to be in control of the expectations within the classroom. The rules that I would recommend are inspired by Linsin (2013):

1. Listen to, and follow all instructions from every adult.
2. When I am teaching a lesson, put your hand up before speaking.
3. Keep your hands and feet to yourself.
4. Respect your teacher, all adults within the school, your classmates and the school itself.

As I said, if you look up Linsin (2013), you will see **very** similar rules. Why these rules? Because to me, they cover every possible infraction within a classroom or the school environment. During my time teaching Primary 1/Reception, I worked in collaboration with the nursery to help plan and support the learning there. One day, a nursery practitioner came to me with her 'hilarious story' of a cheeky individual in her class. She explained that the child had, quite viciously, scratched another child. She further explained that when she confronted the child about the incident, the child pleaded innocence and even referenced the nursery's rules, "But I didn't break any rules. I didn't hit her, I only scratched her." Truth be told, when I looked at the nursery's rules, I agreed (reluctantly) with the child, they hadn't broken any rules – there was no rule about scratching children. Refer back to the rules I suggest above, my favourite rule is the 4th rule, **respect.** For me, this covers everything. If a child headbutts another, they clearly aren't respecting the other and therefore are breaking a rule. Adapt these rules, or other rules so that the system in your class works for you. The only rule I, personally, would avoid having is: "Complete your homework," or words to that effect. We don't always know what family life is like for some of these children. Encourage homework to be completed, support where necessary, but please do not penalise children who are unable to do their homework because of their home life or lack of resources.

You've set your rules, now you have to deal with the consequences of their actions should they choose to break the rules - and remember, it is their choice to break the rules if they want to. You, nor anybody else, can stop them. The only thing you can do is explain the consequences of their actions if they do. Again, inspired by Linsin (2013), I operate an adapted 5-point consequence system, each time they break a rule, they move their name to the next number with an attached consequence:

1. Verbal warning – *this is you telling them that they have broken a rule and they are not to break it again.*
2. Timeout – *they go on a 5-minute time out and are not allowed to return to the class until this is complete. (Please note that you may have to adapt this step depending on the age of your children. Most 10-year old's find the idea of a 'time out' laughable).*
3. 5 Minute loss of free time – *This can be 'Golden Time'; free-play; outside play (whatever is allowed within your school).*
4. Talk to the parents – *Most children worry when you tell them you are going to explain to their parents that their behaviour has not met the expectations today.*
5. Send the child to Senior Management Team to have them talk to them – *Please note: this should be the last of all resorts but you want to avoid doing this regularly unless it is necessary.*

One thing to remember about these rules is that they apply to everyone in the class. You will very quickly learn which children are going to try and break the rules regularly and those who would rarely put a foot out of line. That being said, just because you have a child who doesn't usually break the rules does not mean that they get an additional second chance. That sets a bad precedent for your authority – consistency is key (Plevin, 2016). You must keep everything the same for everyone, similar to being a referee or an umpire – you enforce the rules. I remember in my third straight year teaching Primary 1/Reception when I had my classroom management working exactly how I wanted it to, a child who was always kind and helpful and had never been in trouble decided to hit somebody. At which point, I called her over and she admitted to the infraction. I then told her to move her name to Point-1 on the consequence chart. My busy class suddenly became silent, as they realised that anybody could break a rule and that anybody could receive a consequence.

My final three pieces of advice for teachers is to avoid immediately asking, "Why?" This is, again, inspired by Linsin (2013) in that asking a child *why* they have done something allows them to justify their action. Your job is to find out exactly what has happened – gather the facts. Once you have gathered the facts first, e.g. 'Child 1 punched Child 2, Child 2 then kicked Child 1'. Then you can have a discussion with the children about why this happened or what led to these events and can begin to resolve it, e.g. 'Child 2 took Child 1's toy. Child 1 became upset and hit Child 2, which led to Child 2 retaliating.' By doing this, you separate the actions from the reasons, meaning that the children will eventually receive a consequence after the discussion about their actions in this event, not their reasoning. In this instance, you can then have a restorative conversation with the students, explaining that you understand how they feel and encourage empathy among them. Following this, however, you must make it clear that they have broken the class rules by hitting and therefore will receive a consequence because of their actions. This helps to hold children accountable for the actions while supporting them simultaneously.

Give children the choice if you think they might break a rule: "You can choose to ignore my instruction of 'tidy up' if you want, but if you do, you will be moving your name and receive your consequence". That way, the decision is fully theirs – they know the outcome and the consequence of their action (this works particularly well with younger children).

Finally, **let the children make mistakes.** If you can see from afar that a child is about to break a rule – let them. Let them break the rule and see the outcome themselves for breaking the rule. The simple reason being, you can't punish a child for thinking about breaking a rule, let them break it if they choose to and then they can receive their consequence.

Groupings

Ability groupings are something that many of you will have experienced in your teacher training. Often, you will have arrived at a school and the teacher has already pre-set the groups: the triangle, the square and the circle maths groups. Why do we often make groupings? For simplicity. To streamline and make our jobs easier. Realistically, all teachers are fundamentally aware that each child is at a slightly different level of learning than their counterpart, but to implement as many as 33 different individual learning plans on top of everything else you have to do is simply not practical. Thus, we create groupings.

The notion of groupings, however, isn't without its problems. Often, many classrooms cite particular groups as the 'top group; middle group; or bottom group' (Kress, Jewitt, et al, 2005). This in itself is an issue as it does not support or motivate those who are in the 'bottom' group to strive higher or challenge their learning. It is common that children who start in the 'bottom group' for maths, stay in the 'bottom group' for the rest of their school days (Hargreaves,

2017). As a teacher, it is your job to get the best out of each learner and ensure that they make expanded progress.

The other problem is that teachers often don't, or won't move children's groupings once they are made. In a subject as complex as maths, with various areas of learning within it, a pupil may excel in one area of maths, such as shape or data handling, and require extensive support in another, like numeracy or fractions (Grant, 2019). What this shows, is that teachers cannot keep students within the same maths, literacy or other academic groups, without stifling any potential gains in learning.

This leads us to the notion of 'fluid' or 'flexible' grouping. The idea that groups are interchangeable and will be changing all the time. The idea of fluid grouping is one I would highly recommend for your classroom. It incorporates some of the ideas of 'Mixed-Ability Grouping' (Şalli-Çopur, 2005), but allows the teacher to still use temporary groups to help manage and organise learning or resources. Fluid grouping means that you are constantly assessing your children, to see if you can challenge each child a little further. This means that you could potentially move a child to a different group to meet their learning needs (Conkin, 2010). Optiz (1998) beautifully illustrates the concept of flexible groupings as a sandcastle: something that is built for a temporary purpose and is then washed away and started afresh when finished with.

Please note, that I'm avoiding the use of stating they can move to a "harder" or an "easier" group. I've always tried to teach my class that there's no such thing as 'hard' or 'easy'. Only what is hard or easy to that person. A good analogy I have often used is with numbers, explaining that counting to 10 is 'easy' for them, but might be tricky for a 2-year old child. That doesn't make them more or less smart, it just means that they are on a different part of their learning journey. Embedding this idea was key to children getting on board with the fluid grouping, showing that they can challenge themselves further. It is always exciting to see a child's face when they realise they are doing the same learning as another child whom they thought was 'smarter' than them. That confidence and determination can blossom from this style of grouping.

So, you've heard the background on groupings – now what should you do. As always, check your school's policies on whether they expect it or allow it. Start by conducting a few assessments in your first week at school with your class to determine where each child is in their learning and then you can begin to make your fluid groups. Remember, these assessments are to get a rough estimation of where your children are in their learning. You are then assessing daily to see whether you need to alter their learning path, by providing more challenge or more support. This skill comes with experience but a good way to determine can simply be: can they complete a task independently; independently with some support; with support and feedback; with lots of support; with one to one support; or is unable to complete the task yet.

Find a system that works for you but remember – you are expected to improve and provide opportunities for these learners. Give them that chance.

Short-Term and Long-Term Planning

Planning your curriculum and learning will, most likely, be different from how you planned in your final teacher training post. You would think that every school would do it the same for consistency, but no. There are usually differences.

Your short-term plans are what you intend to do in order to meet certain aspects of the curriculum (Figure 7a & 7b). The purpose of these is to keep you on track with your job of teaching and so that those who are supporting you as a teacher can check what you're doing; give you support if you need it, and to check that you are teaching to the required standard. Having these is also very useful to help guide your day and what you've planned. Most teachers have a daily plan for what their lessons are, but often put less detail into these as they are experienced and usually know what they are doing or what resources they need. I would advise you to be semi-detailed with your weekly plans to ensure you don't forget a key part of your lesson or a resource (trust me, it's easily done).

English:	
Writing	
<ul><li>Imaginative Writing focusing on character development, setting and plot (Introduction of 'Story Mountain'.</li><li>Persuasive Writing – posters, letters, leaflets and radio adverts.</li><li>Discursive Writing – arguments for and against, learn the notion of debate.</li></ul>	
Grammar	
<ul><li>Adjectives, nouns, verbs, adverbs.</li><li>Prefix and Suffix.</li><li>Sentence openers.</li><li>Conjunctions.</li></ul>	<ul><li>Commas and Apostrophes.</li><li>Narrative Voice.</li><li>Present and Past Tense.</li></ul>
Reading	
<ul><li>Fiction – 'Wonder' by RJ Palacio</li></ul>	

Figure 7a – Short/Mid-Term Plans for English

Maths:
• Read, write and order 5-digit numbers, understanding the place value and using < and > signs; add and subtract multiples of 10, 100 and 1000 to and from 5-digit numbers; use written additions to add two 4-digit numbers; work systematically to spot patterns.
• Add and subtract 2, 3 and 4-digit numbers mentally; choose a strategy for solving mental additions or subtractions; solve word problems.
• Understand place value in decimal numbers; multiply and divide numbers with up to two decimal places by 10 and 100; multiply and divide by 10 and 100; add and subtract 0.1 and 0.01; multiply and divide by 4 by doubling or halving twice; use mental multiplication strategies to multiply by 20, 25 and 50.
• Revise converting 12-hour clock times to 24-hours clock times; find a time using minutes or hours later; calculate time intervals using 24-hour clock format; measure lengths in mm and convert to cm; find perimeters in cm and convert cm to m.
• Solve subtraction using a written method for subtracting 3-digit numbers; use counting up (frog jumps) as a strategy to perform mental subtraction; find change from a multiple of ten pounds using counting up.

Figure 7b – Short/Mid-Term Plans for Maths

Schools encourage topics/themes as a vehicle to teach children about the world and reach the other areas of the curriculum to be taught. Which topics you teach changes all of the time. In the years I taught in Scotland, the topic lists went from teachers choosing what they wanted or thought would work best to meet those learning goals, meaning they could teach about the Egyptians or use 'Harry Potter' as a theme; then it changed to being **completely** child-led, meaning that if the children wanted to learn about 'Transformers' or 'Sharks', then that is what was taught (I should also add that the children decided what they wanted to learn within those topics too which meant teachers had to work around them – there are pros and cons to this); and finally, it changed again so topics were advised to only being about things which were directly relevant to the children, meaning that for many areas, topics like 'Ancient Greece' should not be taught as it had no local link to a child in Scotland. This also stated that while children should express their interest and ask questions they would like answered about a topic, it should, again, be the teacher that fully decided the learning. The point is, you need to ask how your school runs with planning topics and themes. You may have an excellent theme or topic that you are passionate about teaching, but your school may not want that taught – and you have to follow your school leader's instructions and orders.

In terms of actual paperwork, you'll more than likely need to keep a file for your NQT year to showcase and track your development. But for your class, you'll probably need to keep a file of your plans too: possibly both short term and long term. I've taught in schools where they want your long-term plans submitted to the leadership team and other schools where the leadership team trust you and your abilities as a teacher to plan effectively. The main thing to remember from all of this is to stay on top of your planning and make sure you are always a few days ahead of yourself (if not more). It will help you to avoid those days of panic.

Some schools may request you to provide weekly plans and evaluations of learning. These can come in a range of formats including online forms or paper templates. These are often used by Senior Leadership Teams to monitor teaching and check on the progress of learners. As always, **ask** if you are unsure of the expectations in terms of paperwork.

Summary of Key Points

- Start your first day as you mean to go on. Show the students **exactly** how they should complete your classroom routines (entering the class, hanging up clothes, handing in homework, etc).
- Practise your classroom routines **continuously**. Do not make the mistake of only practising them for the first two weeks.
- Figure out what works for you and your classroom. Your style of behaviour management must be effective and maintainable. It is imperative that you keep the standards throughout the entire year and hold students accountable for their infractions.
- Groupings will always be a contentious issue. Talk to your school and see what they expect in terms of groupings. I would advise keeping groups fluid and flexible to allow children to be challenged and progress in their learning, as well as be able to move to a group where they can get the support they need if they are struggling.
- Short-term planning should help you manage your day to day lessons and support you in knowing what to do and what resources you need. Long-term planning guides your year of learning and ensures that your class are receiving a broad scope of learning. It will also ensure that you are covering the whole curriculum.

Tip #3

Build Up Those Relationships

Who is in your class?

Your class will likely be made up of the widest variety of children you've ever seen. Children of all shapes and sizes; personalities you connect with and those you find more difficult; a range of skills, knowledge and abilities; and with behaviour which is excellent and trying. I always struggle with my first week with a new class. Purely because I used to compare them to my previous class – big mistake. These children will be very different from your last class. There may be similarities – you may think that 'Child A' reminds you of 'Child B' from your last class, for good or bad reasons. But these children are unique in their own right and must be treated as such, avoid comparing (especially aloud) this class to any other.

Usually, you will get some handover notes from the previous teacher or perhaps even a conversation where they will tell you a little about each child's personality, quirks and academics. They will probably give some additional information about specific children who had behavioural complexities in their class; additional support needs that impact upon their presence in the class; or a medical need which needs to be known about. While it is very important to listen to this advice, as it can help with some preventative measures and supporting particular children, take everything with a 'pinch of salt'.

Why? Because children respond to teachers differently. Children, like teachers, are all different. I taught a particular child in my first year of teaching, whom I was told was 'a nightmare' to teach – he didn't listen, was aggressive to everyone, and was lazy with his work ethic. None of this was apparent while he was with me for a year. Let me point out, this is not because I was an incredible teacher – it was purely because our personalities matched. We had a lot in common and I was able to converse deeply with things he actually liked (sports and video games). The following year, he went to a very experienced teacher (one whom I considered an excellent example of how to be a teacher), and he returned to his aggressive and resistant behaviour. This, again, came down to a personality clash. Furthermore, my early behaviour management skills led to me making life difficult for myself with students. In one class, I received a pupil who I learned had made excellent progress in the previous three years in his behaviour and commitment to learning. It was a revelation. Then he joined my class and everything went wrong. This came down to my teaching style and my personality – it did not match him in any way and I did not adapt appropriately to remedy this situation.

One aspect that you **do** need to listen to, is about social issues regarding the child. I've learned that irrespective of which socio-economic area you work in, children always come with some form of 'baggage'. You should know which children are on the 'Child Protection Register'; which children are 'Looked-After' (possibly by another family member or foster care); which children are from divorced or separated parents (what is the relationship like?); has there been alleged abuse or neglect?

Additionally, you need to know about any medical issues or allergies. This is to ensure that your children do not eat any school dinners that could harm them or to support them with issues they may have in class or at school in general. The most common one I find is Asthma. Check with your school about their policies for having/keeping an inhaler in school/class. Regarding other medical conditions, I would recommend that you contact the parents at the earliest convenience to support the children as best as you can. I recall having a child who had kidney difficulties and required to go to the toilet frequently. I spoke to the previous teacher and the parents to decide how I could best support them. Remember, the routine or support has to work within your classroom and has to be functional for the child. In this instance, the child didn't need to ask me to go to the toilet, they were allowed to go when they needed (but they still had to put the toilet pass on their table so that I knew where they were).

You will learn all about your class in the first couple of months. You will learn who you can trust and who you need to keep an extra eye on; you'll figure out who needs a softer touch at times and who you need to be extremely firm with (though I would argue that you should always be firm but fair). You will learn who daydreams and is not always focused in your classroom; you'll discover who can be challenged and who needs to be nurtured.

How You Develop These Relationships

Over the course of the year, your relationship with the children in this classroom will naturally change. Often, it will start on edge as both you and the children try to figure each other out. They will test your resolve as a teacher and whether you will stand firm on your expectations and boundaries. This is the first part of developing your relationship with them – showing whether you will maintain the structure of the class or let it crumble. This is usually a critical point in how the children (even the usually well-behaved children) will respond to you from then onwards. The classic phrase 'Don't smile until Christmas' is one that is used a lot (Williamson, 2008). Personally, I couldn't do this as I like to smile, be happy and energetic with my class but the notion is that it shows you are serious about their education and that you will stand firm on all areas of your classroom management.

As your class grow with you through the year, you can begin to show sides of your personality much more. You can begin to share those anecdotes from your life which link to their learning, or simply because it's an interesting anecdote (Nickelsen, 2001). You can make those lessons silly or funny. You can make jokes and have a laugh with the children. But remember, you need to be able to return that control immediately from the silly or the funny. For me, this is where I would describe a teacher as having a perfect relationship with their class: able to have fun, be silly, and still get a class back in order and listening fully with a click of your fingers.

I made a mistake in my first year of teaching when I was more focused on being liked that being in control of my class. I may have been the most liked teacher of all time, but as I mentioned before – I had no control of that class. After my first year, I changed my tactic. I adopted the phrase: "I'm not paid to be nice/liked, I'm paid to teach". This simple mind shift allowed me to focus on the fact that I was there to teach these children and to do that, I had to be in control of them before I could build a relationship with my class. The difference this made from my first ever class compared to where I am now with each class is overwhelming.

You will become attached to your class. They will feel like family by the end of the year. But make sure you work the relationship effectively so that it's not a difficult or temperamental family feeling at the end of the year. There is nothing better than that feeling of attachment to your class – you'll know when it's there, I promise.

Difficult Relationships

It is likely that you may have a child in your class whom you do not get on with. Perhaps they continually refuse to follow the class rules and are persistently receiving consequences, or perhaps there is simply a personality clash. Despite this, it is your job to work on and maintain a positive relationship with this child (Sousa, 2009). Maintain the behavioural standards and please do not drop your expectations for that child, but be positive and supportive. Be friendly, kind and funny with them, but ensure that they still receive a consequence if they break your rules.

Despite these children causing you sleepless nights and stressful days, you have to remember two things: first, this child is somebody's little star. This is a parent's pride and joy, somebody they love with all their heart. Remember that when you are bottling up all of your anger towards them. Or occasionally, which is much harder, they might feel there is no-one who loves them with all their heart. Secondly, there may be more beneath the surface of this behaviour. The analogy of a child's behaviour being like an iceberg is forever a relevant idea (Cox and Schopler, 1993; Schopler, 1994). The behaviour that is being exhibited in your class may only be showing part of the problems, emotions or thoughts of this child. Be patient, be open and be empathetic – you don't always know what the child is going through.

SUMMARY OF KEY POINTS

- Remember that this class is **not** the same as your last class – they are different. Try to avoid comparing.
- Use the handover notes from the previous teacher to help you understand any important particulars about children (medical, social, child-protection, behavioural, support needs). But remember to take the social and behavioural elements with a pinch of salt as they may respond differently to you than to their previous teacher.
- Your relationship with your class will grow and change over the year. Enjoy this process.
- It is much more important to be respected as a teacher than liked as a teacher.
- You may have a student that you clash with in terms of your personalities but it is your job to work on that relationship and do everything you can to support that child.
- Remember, there is always a reason for a child's behaviour. Please be sensitive to this, even if it is driving you insane!

Tip #4

Get the Learning Right

What Are Your Class Learning?

Chances are that on your final placement, you arrived in the class and the class teacher gave you their timetable and told you when to teach different lessons: "Monday at 9am is Spelling & Grammar; 10:30am is Maths; 1pm is Topic and 2pm is Music. This was the timetable that you were to adhere to and you, probably, made little to no changes to this timetable as it was not yours to alter.

Now it's different. This is your class and you can do **whatever** you want (within reason). It is common for a lot of teachers to teach Maths and Literacy in the morning (Wragg, 1993), as it's suggested that children are more focused at these times and that these subjects require the most focus. This does not mean that you must teach these subjects at this time. You can teach them whenever you want to – whenever it suits **your** timetable best. Of course, there are some time constraints – break times; lunchtimes; assemblies or specialist subject teachers' timetable – but other than that, you effectively have the freedom to adapt your timetable as you please. In my most recent class, I timetabled all of my reading lessons at 2pm before the children went home. This worked for me as it gave me time to teach the children's reading skills and also allowed me to organise any last-minute memos, letters or notes that needed to go out to parents that day, while they read independently. I've taught Maths at the end of the day and I've taught Spelling in the middle of the day. Find out what suits your personality and style, but also consider how you can get the most from your learners. When or how do they learn best?

While you do have the freedom to experiment with the construction of your timetable, it is (again) important to **ask** your school to see if they have any timetable expectations. Some may expect reading to happen daily, others may want you to have one 'Problem Solving Maths' session per week. The school may also have expectations of how many sessions of each subject there should be per week. It's definitely worth checking. Furthermore, it's important that you balance your subjects across the week. It would not be supportive of the children if you did all five Maths lessons on a Monday and then had no more for the rest of the week. The majority of children require time to practise a skill or knowledge throughout the week, if not longer, and may not achieve this without regular or progressive lessons in class on the subject (Fromberg, 2012; Snow, 2017). This means that while it is probably more productive for you to have daily Maths lessons, you could easily timetable a double Maths lesson for one day, in order to have a day off from Maths. Remember, this is your timetable – you can adapt it if something is not working or if there is a sudden change to your week (perhaps you have an external visitor coming in during your writing lesson that week), you can move that lesson to another time and 'sacrifice' a different lesson instead. You prioritise what you think the children definitely need that week. I once taught in a school where the class I had were displaying large gaps in their Maths, Spelling and Reading abilities. To overcome this, I consulted with my Senior Leadership Team to timetable more Maths and Literacy lessons per week. While this led to less 'topic' or cross-curricular lessons, it meant I had more time to progress and develop some key skills that the children were lacking in their learning.

In terms of lessons, there is often a cliché that experienced teachers will look to you for new and inspired ideas. Please don't take this as added pressure or that you'll be expected to present your lessons to the Local School Cluster – take it as a compliment that experienced teachers want your input in modernising or changing their lesson style. The best thing about this year for you is that you are no longer under persistent scrutiny. Yes, there are observations to ensure you are meeting the required standard. Yes, there will be paperwork to fill in. But in terms of lessons, you can try something out that you've either seen online or heard of before. And if it doesn't work – who cares? You pick yourself up, avoid that lesson again and try something different. Sometimes I would advise you to discuss those disastrous lessons with others, they might have tips for improvement or, at the very least, you will appear human and you'll stop them from making a similar mistake to you. This is your chance to experiment with your teaching style or the conduct of your lessons in the classroom. Have fun with it – try new things. If they were successful, let others know. My favourite thing about primary teaching is that it's all about shared practise. There's no hoarding of materials or refusal to share how best to help children to learn – everyone helps everyone. So, remember to let others know when you've had a good lesson – not in a boastful way, purely supportive.

I've mentioned before that the content of a lesson is derived from your curriculum. Curriculums around the world may be worded differently, but by and large, they all guide the children to do the same thing. They still learn to read, write, spell and solve mathematical problems at around the same ages across all curriculums – no matter what spin you put on it. Different curriculums, however, have slightly different focuses (which change all the time sadly), so you have to ensure that you get these correct. In Scotland, for example, the three core subjects are Maths; Literacy; and Health & Wellbeing. These three subjects are to be interwoven into all lessons in some capacity and should be taught by all teachers (e.g. a P.E. teacher should also teach the class how to spell certain words or do maths games as part of their lesson). This curriculum is also considered to be 'skills-based', in that the teachers should only be teaching the class 'skills' (Scottish Government, 2009). This is different from other curriculums where there can be a broader focus on knowledge; skills; and understanding. In any case, find out what your curriculum is focusing on, check that your content is relevant and then follow through. If you're unsure, **ask** somebody – in my experience, there's always more than one person muddled or unsure (especially in an ever-changing job like teaching). Now, I am fully an advocate of 'Constructivism' in learning, where children help to construct their own understanding of their learning and develop it themselves to enhance their skills and knowledge (Elliot, Kratochwill, et al, 2000). However, sometimes it is imperative that you simply teach the children the content that they need to progress or learn. From time to time, we need to follow a Victorian style of learning by rote and repetition (Lovewell, 2012) for certain subjects to ensure that they are retained. This can be effective for learning things like times tables or spellings of topical words (Reist, 2011).

Finally, at the end of your lesson (as was probably taught to you throughout your teacher training) it's important to have a plenary. A plenary is a short 5-10-minute session at the end of the lesson, to sum up, and check what has been learned or achieved from the lesson. It is important to remember, as suggested by English (2006) that this is a time for students to reflect on their **learning**, not what they have literally done. This often requires training the children to understand what it was they **learned**. You may find at the start of the year, children will say they, "made a poster," when the actual learning was about 'displaying information clearly'. It requires emphasising the learning at the start of the lesson and re-emphasising this throughout the lesson. Often the main aim behind this notion is to show the children that it is a transferrable skill and not unique to that task. Plenaries also don't have to be boring or the same, in fact, I would encourage you to make them as fun as possible. Here are some examples of plenaries I've used (Figure 10), though I'm sure there are many more if you search for them on the internet (please also note that some are more suitable for other age groups):

Examples of Plenaries
- **Exit Pass** – the student can't finish the lesson until they write or draw on a ticket what they have learned from the lesson.
- **Pass the Parcel** (a personal favourite) – Children pass the 'parcel' around to music. When the music stops, the child holding the 'parcel' has to answer a question. To make it more fun, I often have pre-made questions on blue and pink paper so that they can choose the difficulty of their question – "Pink to Make You Think" or "Blue to Challenge You".
- **A Kahoot© Quiz** – An online multiple-choice quiz to see what your children have learned in their lesson. You can even offer Table Points or House Points to the winner.
- **Xs and Os (Noughts and Crosses)** – Play a game of Xs and Os, where the student only gets to make a mark on the game board when they answer a question from your lesson.
- **Guess the Question** – Give your students an answer and see if they can figure out what the question was, based on the learning they have just engaged in.
- **Role Play** – Let a student be the teacher. Have them teach the class how to do the lesson. Have them ask the class questions to check their learning. This is often a fun plenary that children of all ages enjoy doing.

Figure 10 – List of Plenaries that can be done in a lesson

DIFFERENTIATE

Differentiation is now a key part of learning in the primary classroom. Tomlinson and Allan (2000, p4) define differentiation as, "reacting responsively to a learner's needs". This sums up everything that we as teachers must do in the modern classroom. We need to adapt our lessons and the children's learning to ensure that we are meeting their needs. When I first started working in an International School, I was dismayed to hear that some local national schools used very little differentiation and that learners were expected to 'catch up'. For me, it is incredulous to think that I could ever teach a child something that is beyond or beneath their current learning.

So, how do you differentiate? There are many ways that we as teachers can differentiate the learning for learners. I refer back to the fluid groupings mentioned before whereby you can provide different levels of challenge for each group, thereby providing a different level of learning for different children. You can differentiate by the outcome, for example, in writing you may expect different success criteria from different children (Group 1 needs to use at least 3 similes; Group 2 needs to use at least 5 similes). You can differentiate by task – perhaps some children are not ready to write using a pencil independently yet and you offer them to tell their story verbally using a voice recorder. This allows the child to access the learning in a different way which supports them. Finally, you can differentiate by support. It's your job as a teacher to teach and support learners to achieve their goals, but you can also use this as a way to differentiate and challenge students further. You may, for example, give a small group 1-to-1 support or go through the learning with them one question at a time. Whereas another group may receive less support to differentiate the learning.

How you differentiate is very important in class as it allows your children to be supported in a way that helps them the best. Remember, it is your job to help all children reach their individual learning goals. You must provide different levels of support but also different levels of challenge. Just because a child has met the learning goals expected of a child of that age/year-group does not mean that they should stop learning. Push them further onto the next stage of learning.

Learning Styles + Theories

This will just be a short summary; this book is not here to discuss learning styles or theories in depth – there are plenty of other books on that. What I will do, is cover theories and styles that you possibly will use in your practice. Many early-career teachers and student teachers often question the relevance of the theories they were made to learn or state that they hold no merit in the classroom (Barnes, 2017). However, all of these theories and learning styles really do underpin everything we do in the classroom – we just don't think about them explicitly. In other words, you'll never see your mentor or an experienced teacher claim, "I had a great lesson inspired by Vygotsky". But you will use them in some capacity.

The eight main learning styles, postulated by Gardner (1983), are key in thinking about how we teach our class. But before you do that – think about how you learn. Do you learn best independently; in a group; hearing something; reading something? These are things that you will have considered about your own learning, therefore these are relevant and must be considered in your class' learning. **Visual Learners** prefer to learn through seeing or reading images and diagrams; **Auditory Learners** learn best by hearing the learning from things made in rhyme or with rhythm (similar to music); **Verbal Learners** tend to learn best through the words they hear (or read); **Physical Learners** prefer a 'hands-on' approach to their learning, needing active movement or physical activities; **Logical Learners** are usually associated with STEM subjects but are often learners who always need to understand 'why' something happens; **Social Learners**, as the name suggests, prefer learning with other people and often achieve the most success when collaborating; **Solitary Learners**, as a direct opposite to the previous style, are learners who need time by themselves to learn – without distraction from others; and finally, **Naturalistic Learners** are learners who like to be outside and explore the world around them, i.e. children who seem to work best with Outdoor Learning (Diaz, 2019). I should note that these learning styles are not independent of one another, many children often benefit from multiple learning styles for different pieces of learning. Try experimenting to see what works best for each student.

Gosh, that was a long list – but it is important to know and understand these different styles as they could be the key to teaching effectively in your class. Sometimes, upon reflection, we realise that it was not that our teaching was inadequate, it was that we were not meeting the learner's needs. Teaching, as a whole, seems to agree that play-based learning is the best way for children to learn (Bryce-Clegg, 2015; Mead, 2017; White, 2019). However, 'play' is often considered to be a form of 'kinaesthetic' or 'physical' learning (Madej, 2016), which means that you could be neglecting the learning styles of those who prefer visual or auditory stimulus to learn – just something to consider!

In terms of theories, the list is endless. The Learning Styles mentioned above are linked to the theory of 'Multiple Intelligences' (Gardner, 1983), but there are many others that you either use or will use in your class daily. **Cognitivism** (Piaget, 1920) discusses how you need to be aware that your children may acquire skills or knowledge over time, in collusion with other learning opportunities, and not always during your set lesson. **The Zone of Proximal Development**, which is linked to the concept of 'Scaffolding', is concerned with looking at what a learner can do independently and what they can do with support, and by 'scaffolding' their learning to help them achieve their learning goal (Vygotsky, 1978). This is used frequently in classrooms without a second thought from the teachers or supports within the class. The above two theories link well with the notion of '**Constructivism**', which suggests that your learners will build their own understanding of their learning based on their social interactions with yourself and others, or the materials around them (Elliot, Kratochwill et al, 2000). **Bloom's Taxonomy**, you probably remember this one, is a theory which encourages critical thinking and developing knowledge to a higher level (Gershon, 2018). This is a very good model to get on board with and to help plan and improve your lessons, particularly to challenge high-attaining children and your own questioning skills. The **Spiral Curriculum** suggests that complex subjects or learning can be taught and achieved by all children (Bruner, 1960). It explains that by teaching a concept at its most simple level and then regularly returning to it, with added complexity, will gradually improve a learner's understanding and knowledge. Finally, the **Experiential Learning Cycle** (Kolb, 1984) is a theory which encourages teachers to use a cyclical process to support children's learning. It shows that we need to review learning; plan how to improve the learning next time; test the plan of new learning and experience the results; then repeat.

Summary of Key Points

- Sort and adapt your timetable. Remember it can and probably **will** change at some point. Be flexible and make it work for you.
- Try new things – be experimental or creative with your lessons. If they don't work, move on and try something else.
- Ensure you are teaching the correct content. Ask somebody, check with your curriculum and ask an experienced teacher/mentor.
- Differentiate your learning. Remember, not all children are at the same level of learning. Some need challenged, some need support. Get it right for each child.
- Plenaries are important for improving learning (and your sanity). They allow you to check whether children have understood what they were learning to do and whether they can do it.
- Learning theories and styles are very important. While you don't want to think about them or may not see the relevance of them yet, they are always apparent in your teaching (particularly the Learning Styles). Consider how you will vary your teaching and learning to support the different styles of learning.

Tip #5

Keep Your Class Safe

Your Safety – Physical Contact

This is usually the one that strikes fear into most new teachers or teaching students. Often, you are taught to not have any physical contact with a child under any circumstances. Let's look at the facts, yes there have been teachers who have abused students (Canadian Centre for Child Protection, 2018) but they are in the minority. For myself, it just means we have to be wary. The mainstream media can be very critical of teachers and can cause unnecessary fear among teachers, particularly male teachers (Cushman, 2005; Loewenburg, 2017; Cruickshank, 2018), about how close or nurturing they can be towards their students (Jones, 2009). In my experience, this is a very contentious issue because we as teachers **have** to be nurturing and caring, especially when we encounter children who come from a home environment in which there is not sufficient care and nurture to meet their needs. But, as mentioned before, we have to be careful about how and where we show care.

As a rule, I always ensure that I have another adult in view whenever I display any form of nurture or care towards students. As I worked for many years with primarily younger children, the level of physical nurture and care I provided was much higher than when I taught 9-11-year olds. The younger children would often hug me in the morning or would tap me frequently. In the mornings, some children were visibly upset and didn't want to leave their parent/carer so, with parental permission, I would pick them up and carry them in. This was always in clear sight of the parent and when I got to class with them, I would sit them on my knee to calm them down (which they usually did within the first few minutes), again, in full view of another member of staff. Now, I am not in any way asserting that you should just start picking up children or cuddling them. However, sometimes you just know that the child needs a bit of TLC and, often, that is all they need. Knowing that they are loved for, cared for and that you will make things better and look after them is all they need to reassure them. With older children, there is naturally, a higher concern of using any physical contact. However, within reason, you still need to show that you care for these children. We often use 'high-fives' or 'fist bumps' as a way to show TLC with older children but sometimes a 'side-hug' can be used to show care when they're sad or upset about something. At any age, however, do not be the one to initiate the physical contact, where possible avoid it and make sure it is short and in full view of another adult. Understandably, this is a difficult subject (particularly for you, a new teacher), but remember that one of your jobs is to look after your students' emotional wellbeing and that refusing to physically touch them in any way is, arguably, emotional neglect (Winograd, 2009; Hudson, 2019; Carlson, 2020). As ever, **ask** your leadership team (especially if you are working with younger children) and keep yourself safe from any potential allegations.

Your Safety – Technology

Technology has advanced so far that we have lots of it at our fingertips. Literally. Many of you might keep your phones or personal devices very close by in your classroom. Without having to state the obvious – you shouldn't be using your phone while in the presence of children and the children should not have access to anything on your phone (be it a photo, video or app). The difficulty that I have often had, particularly with the younger children, is when something happened in their learning outside that was an excellent example of active or outdoor learning. Some schools have lots of technology, like iPads, which can be taken outside and used to record videos or photos of learning, but sometimes I didn't have anything to hand and, reluctantly did use my phone to capture the achievement or learning. The agreement with staff at some schools was that their phones could be inspected at any time should they have to use their phones for a photo/video and that they are only to use them if no other recording device was available. As advice to you, **avoid** using your phone – find another device to use. It means that you can't put yourself in a difficult situation or leave yourself open to allegations from children.

Linked to the use of your own devices is the use of the school devices. Often a school will provide you with a laptop for in-class teaching, usually connected to some form of interactive whiteboard and possibly even a tablet device (depending on the resources your school has available to you). First, remember that you are borrowing these devices and that you must look after them. Secondly, where possible, try to use them purely for your work. Most school devices will flag up any inappropriate searches, whether you are on the school internet or your internet at home – so be considerate of what you are searching for on **any** school device.

Your Safety - From Children

Sadly, there are some instances where you must protect yourself from some children. The children in your class or your wider school community all have a variety of histories which have affected who they are as people now and also how they react.

Firstly, avoid being left alone with a student at any time. In doing so, you leave yourself open to the possibility of unwanted allegations from the child – without a witness to support your defence should these allegations be false. Some children, as a way to manage their chaotic world, develop a pattern of lying which often begins as a way to escape the reality of their life or gain attention from someone. Unfortunately for some, as they get older, lying can become innate to them. If you learn there is a child with a history of telling lies you must be extra vigilant and have another adult present if you ever have to speak to that child alone in class, possibly about an infraction. Keep yourself safe and leave no opportunity for allegations to be made.

Some children display angry or violent behaviours at school. This can derive from an array of reasons, ranging from circumstances at home, to personal and social issues, to bullying within the school or an additional support need (Radford, 2012). If there is a child in your classroom with a history of extreme emotional or violent behaviour, then they will probably have an Individual Plan on the best strategies to support them - these will vary from case to case. These will usually be discussed with you before you meet that child.

However, something to be aware of is that children who do not necessarily have an extreme history can still become emotional and react violently. In most instances if you have developed a relationship with the children in your class you will be able to pre-empt that something is not right and be ready to respond or, hopefully, defuse a situation but rarely will you know what exactly you will be responding to that day. It is, therefore, good to have these general points in the back of your mind because when you respond you need to do so fast.

First things first: make sure that the rest of the children are safe. If you have to evacuate the class, do it. Secondly, make sure that the child in question is as safe as possible without putting yourself in serious harm's way but do not restrain them unless you are level three CALM (Crisis, Aggression, Limitation and Management) trained. Thirdly, get help. If you have a child with a history of extreme violent behaviour, you will probably already have another adult with you, however, this is not always the case nor is it the case for children who have unexpectedly erupted. Send another child to the nearest classroom and contact a member of senior management who will come to help diffuse these situations.

Sometimes, when a pupil becomes upset, angry or aggressive as well as becoming violent, they may also try to escape. In these instances, you should never block an exit from a child. They always need to have a way out. If they don't have an escape, often what can happen is they take their built-up aggression out on you, the furniture or the other children. This book is not here to terrify you, some of my colleagues have never experienced more than a mild playground scrap. However, I do know many colleagues who have experienced violent incidents with multiple children in their care. As a couple of small varied examples: I know one teacher who experienced being assaulted or intervening when others were assaulted weekly from the same child; another teacher who regularly experienced a child soiling themselves in defiance; some teachers who have had to deal with children deliberately bringing weapons to school and I know several colleagues who've had to evacuate classrooms due to various students having aggressive difficulties. Again, this is not written to frighten you, only to showcase some of the varying things that can happen in a classroom.

The main thing to take away from this is to be understanding. Yes, you may encounter scary situations with some children in your teaching practice, but please remember: they are **children**. They can be just as frightened as you, which often leads to this behaviour. Normally, before you get a child with behavioural difficulties in your class, you would receive some notes about things that work and things to avoid doing. But remember to **ask** for help with children who are violent or aggressive and keep yourself safe.

Pupil Safety (History & Chronology)

The children you receive in your class will come from the widest range of backgrounds with the widest range of stories possible. You may learn about some children with troubling histories in which they have been exposed to a number of different categories of abuse or their families have been devastated by illness or loss. Your main priority is to ensure that all the children in your class are safe, both inside and outside your classroom. When you receive your class, you will, usually, be informed of any relevant history about the child. This could be knowing that the child was a victim of drug and alcohol abuse; learning that they live with a grandparent and do not see their biological mother or father; physical abuse at home; neglect; extensive academic pressure on the child. The list is endless.

I should note that we cannot, and should not, make assumptions about any children based upon the area they live in. Just because you teach in what might be considered a 'rough' area, does not mean that there will be children being abused or neglected any more than children from an affluent area. Neglect and abuse come in many forms – you need to be aware of this. I've worked in many different socio-economic areas. In each area, I have seen examples where children were neglected physically (they arrived at school with dirty clothes and usually unfed), or emotionally (usually they didn't see their parents as they were always working and the parents would show them very little love or care). Both of these can be very damaging for the children in your class.

Another really important factor to consider is to avoid making assumptions based on the family. I recall teaching a child who was from a very nice family with no history of social work or police involvement. One day this child showed up with huge bruises all over their limbs. I could have thought, 'There won't be a problem, not with *this* family' and immediately dismissed the bruising. But as a teacher, you must be critical. You must still ask the child what happened. You must still explain that you can't keep a secret and that you have to tell somebody about it. I followed my Child Protection Policy and informed my Child Protection Officer. Thankfully, on this occasion, it turned out that it was not abuse. Again, ensuring that you do not make assumptions about families or children can be the difference between a child being safe or not.

Sometimes, the problems aren't always clear and there doesn't seem to be clear evidence of abuse or a problem. This is where a 'chronology' (Figure 8) can be useful. Some schools have them as standard practise, others are only used by certain teachers. I would highly recommend creating a chronology to help keep notes on **every** child in your class. You never know when it might be important to a child's case. I would often write anything in the chronology that was out of the ordinary:

- "Child A has arrived at school with a black eye, said they ran into a tree";
- "Child B cried for 1 hour in a corner, unable to explain why they were upset";
- "Child C scratched Child D during play";
- "Child E soiled himself today".

The latter example proved vital in a Social Work case that my colleague was involved in. After recording this child's regular 'accidents' in class and comparing these to social work records and police reports of recorded incidents within the home, they learned that 'accidents' always happened in conjunction with the other agencies' reports. As a result, changes were able to be made more quickly to support and safeguard this child.

Child Z			
<u>Date</u>	<u>Event</u>	<u>Comments/ Remarks</u>	<u>Signed</u>
13/11/2022	Child Z has arrived at school with dirty clothes for the past three days.	See event on 03/09/2022	M.WATSON

Figure 8 – Example of a Chronology

One key thing to remember about a chronology is that it is there to keep track of the **facts** – not your inferences. When writing a chronology, you write down <u>exactly</u> what has been said or happened, note the time and place. If another adult saw or heard what happened, <u>they</u> write it in. It is not your job to infer that Child F stole food because his sister steals his food. It is your job to write down that, "Child F stole food from Child G". If the child makes a verbal statement, then you can write that down too, "Child F said that he was hungry because his sister stole his breakfast". These chronologies are here to help keep your children safe – use them to your advantage.

CLASSROOM SAFETY (POLITICAL/RELIGIOUS/SOCIAL) MESSAGES

Within your class, you will likely encounter moments where particular political, religious or social messages are at the forefront of discussions or teaching. It is imperative, however, that your personal views remain impartial and balanced; and that you teach both sides of the divide fairly.

A common one to be discussed, particularly in the latter stages of Primary, is politics and social ethics. Often, Primary students are not fully knowledgeable about current politics in their country. They may know of certain politicians but much of their knowledge will usually come from their parents passing comments. The difficulty you have is ensuring that you are balanced in your discussion of policies or politicians. A child may come from a family which particularly supports one political party. If you denounce that party leader and policies, then you are immediately open to complaints. Issues that arise from politics should be discussed in a balanced manner to allow learners to make their own decisions. An example I could use would be the October 2020 British Parliament's vote on whether to continue to provide children with 'Free School Meals' during a pandemic. As a teacher, it is my job to ensure that I do not share my views (so as not to influence the learners). It is vital that I share the reasoning as to why some feel children needed the Free School Meals but also why many of the politicians voted against the 'Free School Meals.' This is to allow children to make an informed decision. It is suggested that children are very impressionable with our views as teachers (Wendling, 2007), and therefore it is vital that we maintain an unbiased stance and put the children's views into the spotlight instead.

Generally, most people would state they believe racism to be wrong (MacKinnon and Fiala, 2018), however, we still have to maintain a balanced and unbiased approach to our practice. Now, I am not advocating the promotion of racist, xenophobic or sectarian attitudes. But it is important to discuss **why** some people have these attitudes but also to explore the problems with these attitudes. Why do some people dislike other people based purely on their race or nationality? Why is this a problem? Rather than simply stating racism is wrong, you have to explore this problem with them.

The other issue which regularly arises is the issue of religion. In the multi-cultural society that we live in today, we must be accommodating of other faiths and creeds. For the majority of students, religious persecution will be easily taught as a negative element of life. However, there may be some students with particular backgrounds who are not accepting of some faiths. This can be as broad as the conflict between Palestinian Muslims and Israeli Jews; and the historical feud between Catholics and Protestants. In the classroom, it is your job to present the information to students – not to convert them. Everybody has a belief system whether that is through identifying as a particular religious group or choosing not to partake in faith groups, whatever your personal belief system, your teaching and discussions surrounding faith and religion should always be impartial. You are tasked with informing learners about the variety of religions and beliefs from around the world and, in some cases, to dispel some stereotypes, prejudices or inaccuracies that students have about particular faiths or religions.

Another problem which may occur is where particular students are withdrawn from your Religious Education lessons. Parents withdraw their children from lessons on religions for a variety of reasons, though usually, it is to do with a parent's concerns with another religion or a parent's fear that the teacher does not know enough about their religion to teach it accurately (Smalley, 2018; Busby, 2019). In the instance that a parent withdraws their child from Religious Education, I would speak to your Senior Leadership Team for advice and then arrange a short meeting or phone call with the parents. The main thing you want to get across to parents is that you are teaching, **not** preaching. You are not trying to convert any child to any faith or religion – simply to inform them of the facts; customs, values and routines of different religions. Many children see various people in society and have various questions. In school, it is our job to fill those gaps in education and answer those questions. Should the parents still decide that they want their children withdrawn from these lessons, ensure you provide their child with an appropriate independent task for them to complete while you are teaching the rest of the class.

SUMMARY OF KEY POINTS

- Consider what physical contact you give to any children (whether it is a high-five, fist bump or a side hug). Are you required to show more nurture and care for young students? Discuss this with your senior leadership team.
- Be considerate of the technology you have been given from the school. Take care of the laptops or tablet devices, etc. Also, consider what you are searching for on the internet using these devices – many schools/local authorities have the right to search your computer at any time for anything inappropriate.
- Be aware of students' violence or aggression. Learn to build a relationship with any children who have these difficulties so that you can support them to calm down.
- Ensure you have the relevant history of children with violent behaviour and contact your Senior Leadership Team if there are any concerns for the safety of yourself or any children.
- Maintain an unbiased approach to your teaching and be sensitive to political, social or religious content and practices.
- Be aware of all types of abuse and remember that abuse can happen everywhere.
- Use chronologies to keep track of any events which are significant or out of the ordinary for children in your class.

Tip #6

What Is Expected of You

Things You Should Be Doing

This might sound obvious, but you are expected to teach a class. Within each NQT/Probation year, there are different requirements, expectations and supports. However, most of these are similar enough to allow me to generalise.

Most schools, councils and authorities in the UK allow new teachers one day off per week or a reduced timetable. This day off as a new teacher is a blessing. You will likely be exhausted and have a million things to catch up on. However, this 'day off' is not a day for you to have no work to do and relax. It is a day to improve yourself as a teacher. Yes, you may have the odd day where you catch up on your marking and finally make that display you've been planning for the last fortnight, but this 'day off' should be used more practically. These days out of class are an excellent opportunity to visit other classes in the school and see how their teacher manages the class (possibly even for the whole day). It's a chance to visit other schools and see how they operate. I would encourage you, where feasible, to visit as many schools as possible on your day out of class. Doing this will give you a greater perspective of education within the council or local school group but will also introduce you to ideas you had never considered. I'm a bit of a nosey teacher. I love going into other teacher's classrooms. Never to critique, but purely to steal as many amazing ideas as I possibly can to improve my practice. I recall speaking to a Head Teacher who occasionally received a request from an NQT/Probationer teacher to visit their school to observe a teacher. The Head Teacher told me that they always tried to send the NQT/Probationer to a teacher who they knew were using successful approaches which were unique or different to approaches used by others within that school. This often means you will have a chance to expand your ideas and see some excellent teaching practice to model your teaching upon thereafter. Additionally, there are often various courses that are available to teachers which you should try to register for to develop your practice. Many of these courses are also now available digitally, meaning you can access more, without it impacting upon your teaching day too much.

Furthermore, your day out should also be used to research ways to improve your practice. Many of you will begin planning your lessons and will get into the routine of how these lessons are structured or completed for the remainder of the year. But as an NQT/Probationer, this is your chance to experiment with some new ideas. Explore different methodologies of teaching. There may be a method that you've never seen before – learn about it and try it. It might be one of the most successful methods out there and nobody has used it in your school yet. You could be that practitioner to help improve the entire school's practice. If you have tablets or technology available in the school, learn how to use them so that you can teach the children or use them as a tool to improve your practice. You'd be amazed at how many practitioners struggle with using technology in their classroom when there are so many useful applications to improve or excite learners.

This time out of class is also a good time to ensure that you are up to date with your school planning. As I mentioned previously, schools usually plan in different ways and have different expectations. I recall talking to a fellow NQT/Probationer about the differences in our schools planning expectations during our NQT/Probationer year and I was amazed at how different they were. Considering the fact that we were both doing the same job, our workloads were very different in terms of planning. Use the occasional day to make sure you are up to date and that you have filled things out properly.

As an NQT/Probationer, you will have paperwork to document your journey and progress towards being fully qualified. You should have been assigned a mentor to support you during your first year so ensure that your paperwork is up to date on your day off. This is a good time to ensure your reflections are recorded and sent to your mentor. As many of you will complete your first teaching year in different cities and regions, the expectations of you as an NQT/Probationer change. Local councils may vary and have different expectations on top of the expectations from the national authority. You might not be able to meet your mentor on or during your day out of class, but you should ensure that you have all your resources and paperwork prepared for when you do liaise with them. You should also ensure that you do get time with your mentor. Your mentor will usually be a fellow teacher who you will see regularly, but it is still important to have scheduled discussions with your mentor which are more purposeful than a casual chat. Sometimes, your mentor will be a member of the Senior Leadership Team. This isn't usually a problem and can happen if no teachers are willing to be an in-school mentor. The biggest flaw, however, is that members of the Senior Leadership Team are busy individuals and they can, unintentionally, miss observations or meetings with yourself. If you have a member of SLT as your mentor, ensure that you do get your regular meetings and observations from them. It is vital to your development.

COMMITMENT

When I think about the schools I have worked for, I always relate it to sports teams I support. I work for that school and I will support them like I support my favoured sports team. But the question is, how committed are you to your school? Are you offering these children the best education possible? As a class teacher, you should be committed to improving your practice at every available opportunity. Figuring out what has worked and being committed to developing those areas which are not working. Are you committed to completing all of the relevant paperwork that you have? You will likely have paperwork to do as an NQT/Probationer on top of your paperwork as a class teacher – are you committed to getting it done properly, or are they all half-hearted jobs completed at the last minute? Your effort in these areas will always be seen by members of your leadership team so please consider this.

How much time are you putting into your job? Are you arriving 5 minutes before the start of school and leaving as soon as the children go home? While there is technically nothing wrong with this, it does raise questions about your commitment and professionalism. Yes, there will be days where you have an appointment or you are simply exhausted and need to go home. But be sensible about things. Some of you might already have children of your own or be a registered carer for somebody and therefore do not arrive at school as early as others or may have to leave school soon after your class goes home. In this instance, ensure that being away from school doesn't affect your workload. You may have to take more work home to complete it there, rather than in the school building – but make sure it works for you and your family. In these instances, I would advise that you make your Senior Leadership Team aware of your family and childcare circumstances as they may be able to support you further.

Another common issue raised about 'commitment' is often about teachers' absences. Firstly, if you are ill, you should not be at school. That's about as clear as I can be. However, especially around the winter months, everyone gets a sore throat, everyone gets a cold. It's whether these ailments are enough to stop you from physically doing your job or not. I've had colleagues continue to come to work even when they had no voice left, which I can assure you is an almost impossible task when you cannot shout over rambunctious children! Linked to illness, though I consider this to be self-inflicted and therefore not an illness would be midweek drinks. Meeting with friends, family or colleagues for a meal or drinks midweek is allowed

– it's your free time after all. But please be wary of the morning after. Are you going to be hungover? If you're too hungover then you will end up taking an absence which doesn't show commitment to your job. Consider your commitment to your school and your role as a teacher.

This question of commitment, however, goes beyond the simplicity of, 'Are you teaching these children as best you can?' Schools are often so integral to a local community that they require a presence during various events. Throughout the year, your school will host or be a part of various events: concerts or fayres; school discos; festivals; the list is endless. How many of these are you helping at? As an NQT/Probationer, I would say that you should try to be at as many as possible. I understand that many of these events happen in the evenings or at the weekends, and sometimes, yes, you will be unable to attend. Usually, these events are organised well in advance so you should have plenty of notice to know whether you can attend or not. But do consider it, this kind of commitment always puts you in good stead. Furthermore, there are commitments to your school that you can show in terms of school development. Are you offering to help lead or support a working group? Is there something you can offer to the school to help develop it? We have previously talked about your expertise or individual skills as a practitioner - could you use these to develop a policy or area of the curriculum to progress the school?

Parent Council, or whatever mismatch of words your school uses for their parent liaison group, is often something that many teachers have no desire to be involved in. The groups that I have attended have often been fairly irrelevant to me as a practitioner but there usually has to be a teacher representative at the meetings. So, if you're free, why not volunteer yourself to be that person? Usually, the meetings are about the problems within the school so it's a great way to find out more about your school but is also a good way to meet more of the 'key' parents in the school (though, if you're helping out at events in the school, you'll usually have met these parents already!).

Are You Listening?

I remember when I passed my degree. It was one of my proudest achievements. I also recall my final teaching placement, which went very well. I would say it was a great success – I knew what I was doing and I felt like an expert. This was my first mistake. Despite all you have learned in your teacher training, there is still so much more to learn, and you have to be ready to listen to what everybody says to improve things. I remember receiving advice from colleagues and not using it; getting hints from my mentor and basically ignoring it; being, effectively, told to do something by a member of the leadership team and not doing it; all because I felt I knew better.

Needless to say, I was wrong. My first year was an unmitigated disaster. I should have listened to my colleagues when they wanted to help me. By the time I had learned to keep my mouth closed and listen, it was too late to salvage a pass for my NQT/Probation year. Now, I'm not here to say that everything a colleague or a mentor tells you, is the best thing to do. They may be a little 'old fashioned' in their methods, they may have little experience in your age group or they may suggest something that you completely disagree with. Either way, still think about it and still consider it. Often, teachers or mentors will just give you advice, without you asking. They've been in your situation and don't want you to make the same mistakes they made (much like this book!). It is up to you whether you follow their advice or not, but one thing you should never do is ask for direct advice and then ignore it. If you ask for direct advice on how to do something or improve a lesson, then follow the advice they give you. A teacher is always going to give you the best advice they can. Blatantly ignoring this advice will not put you in good stead with that teacher.

Summary of Key Points

- Your day out of class is not a day off. Use it effectively.
- Ensure you find time to meet with your mentor – especially if they are in a Senior Leadership Role. Make it happen by hook or by crook.
- Show commitment to your job by ensuring you do everything to the best of your ability.
- Show commitment to your school by trying to engage with and support the school in their in-school developments or external school events.
- Listen to the advice you get from colleagues or mentors.
- Follow their ideas, whether you like them or not. If they don't work, then you don't have to continue with them.

Tip #7

You're a Professional, Act Like It

You Are Now a Celebrity

Okay – let's just get one of the big ones out of the way first: Social Media. Chances are that most of you have some form of social media account. This means that students and parents **will** search for you (and could request to add/follow you). Johnson (2019) even inferred that parents should investigate you as a teacher on your social media and see what you get up to, to check if there are any fallacies in your personal life. This notion in itself is reason enough to not allow parents and children access to your social media.

One thing to consider is a parent's views on how you live your personal life or what you get up to. Something as simple as a political view could stir up unneeded trouble with parents who have a particular stance. Within this, even consider things like your 'profile picture' – does it have a particular political party emoji or sticker on it? Could parents see that? Could they have an issue with this? Do you support a certain sports team? I can think of a few cities where this could be a rather big issue for some parents. The list is endless. That doesn't mean that you can't post pictures of your nights out at the pub – just that you should think about any photos displaying you in a compromised position. All I'm suggesting is to consider **what** you post, or others post about you, on social media. Is there a photo of you doing something that could be deemed as sexually explicit or wearing something that reveals a bit too much? Again, I am not telling you how to run your social media – only tips to keep parents (or students) from getting near it to have **anything** against you. You want to maintain a professional relationship with these parents and give them no reason to dislike you. As a result, I try to keep my personal social media as opinion-free as possible. I post photos of my holidays and any large social gatherings (weddings, etc). In fact, I try to avoid even commenting on public messages (Facebook groups etc) just in case parents follow the same groups and disagree with my views. Now, I should end on a slightly less dreary note. The majority of parents are not out to get you and do not want to see you fail. Many will search for you on social media out of pure curiosity. They see how great you are with their children and how friendly you are to them that they just want to extend their social group to somebody nice. Or, as I've found, some people just 'add/follow' **anybody** they've ever met – and don't think about the ramifications. Usually, this was always a cut and dry scenario for me – don't speak to or add parents or children on social media. However, sometimes there are circumstances which may allow it and often this happens in smaller towns where 'everyone knows everyone'. In one school I taught at, many of the teachers were already friends with many of the parents before they were teachers – meaning they were already friends on social media. In this instance, it is your call as to whether you can maintain this relationship on social media while you are teaching their child, though often it's not considered a problem. I've also seen some teachers set up a 'class account' so that parents can contact teachers on social media for ease of access (though, this is something that would definitely need to be checked with by your Senior Leadership Team).

Depending on where your school is, you may encounter children or parents from your class outside of school. In this instance, remember that to them, you are still a teacher. You are still the professional in charge of their child and you have to maintain this professionalism, even though you're off the clock! Usually, a simple 'Hello! How are you? What are you up to today? Right, I must be going,' is suffice conversation for most children and parents that you meet outside of school but you can gauge the situation appropriately. I have on occasion run into a parent at a restaurant, a bar or met a parent in a supermarket when I had alcohol in my trolley. Some teachers have the fear that if a parent saw them with alcohol, that their entire career would crumble. This is not the case, most parents understand that you are entitled to a bottle of beer or a glass of wine. Some may even strike up a conversation and say that, "you've earned it after having to deal with that class all week," (this is a verbatim conversation I had with a parent I met in a bar). There may be the odd parent who thinks that you should be the most angelic example of a human being possible, but I wouldn't worry about them. The main thing is to ensure that you maintain the standards set for yourself as a professional. Stumbling around vomiting from extreme intoxication when you are aware of multiple parents in the nearby area might not look very good for you as a teacher – especially as parents talk. As mentioned in the sub-title, you're a celebrity so people will want to know everything about you and there will be gossip. Make sure that the gossip is positive.

You Have a Boss – Remember That

When you start your new teaching job, most of you will keep yourselves to yourselves, focusing more on making sure that you are caught up with all your marking and ensuring that those learning displays are perfect. However, as you start to make friends and develop trust with your colleagues, the staff room can become a place to rant. And as I will mention in this book, having a good rant or moan about things in the school is important – getting things off your chest is a good way to relieve the stress of teaching ("How many different ways can I tell them to stop talking?"; "Child X didn't follow instructions *again* meaning I had to explain it all for them *again*,"; "I have *so* much marking to do, I literally can't be bothered. They can mark it themselves.") The occasional good rant or chat is good for morale.

At some point, however, a teacher will likely rant about the leadership team. They might complain about a decision they've made; a new system that they've implemented; complain about the way they spoke to them in a meeting, or make a personal attack on their appearance or manner. You must stay out of these conversations and rants. At the end of the day, whether you agree, disagree or are part of the rant, the members of the leadership team are your bosses and you must give them that respect. Yes, you may disagree with them on something and you might even dislike them. But keep that to yourself. By opening up your opinions to others, you risk being pulled up for professionalism standards by the leadership team. I have heard of individuals being pulled up for ranting on social media about their leadership team; I have read about entire groups of teachers being pulled in for a discussion about their inappropriate conduct. Many teachers often forget that their leadership team are their bosses and that they must follow their lead, whether they like it or not.

There may be some things that are implemented that you think will not be a good idea or that you are concerned about. Talk to your leadership team and explain your concerns or why you think their decision needs to be adapted or changed. Moaning or making inappropriate comments, especially behind their back, will not change the problem.

Summary of Key Points

- Be wary of what you display or post on social media. Parents and students will search for you.
- Be polite when you meet students or parents in public, but remember to maintain your professionalism.
- Remember that your Head Teacher or Leadership Team are your bosses and you do have to do what they tell you, whether you believe it is a bad idea or not.

Tip #8

Parental Guidance

Who Are Your Parents?

Parents. To some teachers, the mere word 'parents' sends shivers down their spines. To others, it's an enjoyable relationship to share, watching their child grow throughout the years. But what is a parent's role in their child's education?

Well, arguably, their role is bigger than yours in the education of their child. A parent should be valuing the importance of education from the beginning. Parents should be setting good standards of behaviour and manners, for their children from the beginning. Parental involvement and support are key to ensuring the success of all children in your class (Slavin, Madden, et al, 2009). However, not all parents are the same. They vary as much as the children in your class. And much like the children in the class, the area that they are from does not denote their social or financial status.

Some parents will be experienced, with several children and are very understanding of your job. Some parents will be very new to parenting and will find it hard to let their child go. Some parents will be wealthy and can afford to give their child a nutritious lunch, expensive and worthwhile clothing and exciting toys to play with. Some parents will barely scrape through the week financially. Some parents suffer from substance abuse and some are single parents. For the most part, you won't know everything about every parent. But it's important to try and get a feel for the different parents in your class. It also allows you to know who is at home with the child in your class – who is in their immediate social circle and who influences them the most? Is there potentially a detrimental influence at home? These are things to consider, especially when you consider the impact the child could have on your class as a result.

You often tend to meet parents on a more regular basis that have children aged 4-7 years old. After that age group, you tend to see parents on fewer occasions; unless, sadly, it is for negative reasons.

Supporting Parents

As teachers, part of our role now is to support parents (Schlechty, 2011). Parents require support in a variety of manners and it is your job to support them, where appropriate.

Academics is something that your parents will all have a wide and varied background in. Some of the parents you teach will have a university or college degree and will have already begun teaching their children. Some parents have had a difficult relationship with education due to their own experience and may not give their children or you the support needed from the beginning. Some parents simply don't have the knowledge to be able to support their children. That's not a critique or a personal attack – simply a note from experience and research. When children reach a certain age, many parents begin to struggle with the content that is being taught (Jackson, 2004; Aggor, 2014). Some parents simply cannot give the academic support that their children need to succeed in their homework. In the UK alone, it is suggested that more than 20% of adults suffer from some level of illiteracy (National Literacy Trust, 2017) meaning they may only be able to help with their child's education up to a certain age.

So how do you support them? First, ensure you have an open communication line with the parents about what their children are learning and what they need to do for their learning at home. Often, I try to keep things as simple as possible for any homework – learn your multiplication tables; learn your spelling words/phonemes, but there may be times where you may need to provide slightly more complex learning for homework. This is where you have to be flexible and open with parents as they simply may not understand what to do. Additionally, the students may not have the resources at home to complete this homework. A classic example was where I set an entire year group a homework task which included doing some research online about the design of album covers for classic rock bands. While this sounds like a fairly simple internet search task, my Learning Assistant highlighted that some children do not have access to the internet at home. This is something I had never considered as a possibility in 2015, but there it was. I adapted my homework to support the children **and** the parents: I allowed those students who could not do their homework at home to complete their homework in school. They were not forced to do this, they were given the opportunity to complete it in their own time. Another option is to create a 'Homework Club'. These clubs look different in every school, but the best ones, in my view, are the ones where teachers are there too. Having teachers there with the children and the parents, allows the parents to receive non-judgemental support from the teachers about **how** to complete the homework and tips for completing it more effectively at home. There are many other ways that you can help the parents during these conversations too, you just have to be there to offer!

The reality of modern-day teaching is that you may be in your early twenties with minimal life experience and are being asked for advice on parenting by somebody older than you – I have experienced this. When this happens, be honest. If you can offer a helpful or informed suggestion, then do. If you can't, then find a more experienced teacher who can offer that parent support. Sometimes parents just need somebody to relay the common sense to them or to tell them that they are doing a good job. I've had parents come to me in tears (which I can assure you is rather harrowing) pleading for help because they don't know what to do. Sometimes, all you need to do is remind the parents to give their child a bedtime; make sure they have a snack or the correct clothing; to have a routine in place for when they break the rules at home.

Sometimes, parents need support with their children's behaviour. They see and hear that they are well behaved in your classroom and yet they are difficult at home. Offering behaviour support is difficult because, as teachers, we can disassociate ourselves emotionally and can cope with a child who is upset when they have broken a rule. This is different for parents as they will love their child unconditionally. Many parents struggle to discipline their child as either: they hate to see their child crying and upset (Silverman 2004) or they have not established authority at home (Taffel, 2012). In general, keep your behavioural advice to parents as simple as possible: be firm and follow through on your actions.

Dealing with Parents

As I mentioned before, most parents are truly wonderful and very much appreciate everything you have done for them and their child. Other parents, however, appear determined to make things as difficult as possible for you. In my career, I've only had a minimal number of 'difficult' parents but have plenty of colleagues with numerous horror stories. When dealing with upset parents, first things first – do not entertain any conversation if a parent is extremely aggressive or shouting at you. Also, if you have a class of children in your care, for example, first thing in the morning when you are taking the children into school, the children are your priority. Politely direct the parent or guardian to the office to make an appointment with yourself or Senior Leadership.

When you come to addressing any parental concern, make sure you know all the facts regarding any problem. If you don't know everything to do with a particular problem, then explain to them that you will look into what has happened from multiple sources before discussing it with them further. **Then go and do that.** Find out what actually happened from multiple sources and report back to the parent. When you report back, try not to use any other children's names, keep it as diplomatic as possible and, most importantly, be **honest, firm** and **fair**. It is your job to be unbiased and tell the parent(s) what has happened and, following your classroom management plan and school behavioural policy, hand out the consequences. Some parents, sadly, are convinced that their child can do no wrong and will not accept any evidence you present to them (a colleague of mine was called a 'liar' by a parent when she explained that the entire class, the learning assistant and herself all witnessed the child in question punch another) but stand by what you have said and do not waiver when parents get loud. If they are unwilling to accept your decision then send them to the leadership team and they will deal with it.

As a result of the above problems, I always advise you to keep additional notes of these issues on top of anything you put in your chronology. By doing this, you can simply hand your notes to the leadership team who can use this when they talk to the parent.

Ideally, when you have a problem to deal with, you will phone the parent and the problem can be dealt with over the phone without requiring a meeting. In some schools, they use apps or emails to message the parents with any problems or concerns. These are all really useful ways to deal with minor problems or concerns without having to inconvenience the parents too much. However, when dealing with more serious complaints, concerns or problems, you will often need to speak to the parents in person. When you arrange a meeting, find an appropriate place for your conversation, possibly your classroom or a designated room within the school. It is very important that you feel comfortable when you speak to the children's parents. You might be nervous the first few times but you need to be comfortable with the discussion you are having. If it is a serious discussion, then I would advise having an additional person there with you (depending on the severity, usually a member of the leadership team should be there). There may be a parent who has had frequent complaints or problems and, therefore, it would be advised to have an additional person there. Finally, and most importantly, take notes of what has been said, additional details and, most importantly, the next steps to resolve the problem.

As a rule of thumb, I always encourage teachers to summarise the notes they have taken during the meeting with parents. Read your summary to the parents and check that they agree with what has been noted down and what has been decided going forward. This allows you to ensure that everyone agrees with the notes and that parents cannot claim that something was not discussed with them.

Summary of Key Points

- Figure out what kind of parents you have in your class.
- Be open with parents and support them if they have academic difficulties.
- Create opportunities (such as homework clubs or lunch-time homework) to allow children to complete their homework at school when they can't do it at home.
- Some parents need help with 'parenting', offer them help where you can. If you don't know what to say, recommend another teacher who may have better experience or support for them in their concerns.
- Be firm, honest and fair with all complaints from parents.
- Try to deal with as many problems as possible over the phone.
- Some problems cannot be dealt with over the phone as they are much more serious. In these cases, I would always advise having an additional person there as a 'witness'.
- Take 'minutes' or notes of every meeting you have, in case you have to refer to them later. At the end of your meeting, quickly summarise everything that has been said to ensure that the parent agrees with what has transpired.

Tip #9

Find a Friend

Help!

Inevitably in your job, like any profession, you will need help. This may not be excessive help, but it is still helpful to know who you can go to for some non-judgemental advice. You will be spending nearly a third of your weekdays with the people in your school, so it's really important that you try to find a friend in school. Somebody who you can bounce ideas off of; somebody to chat to during break and lunchtimes; somebody you can have a laugh with when times get tough!

Through this friend, you can ask for tips on how to get your class to learn; how to get children to behave properly; how to make your lessons more exciting; how to handle the pressure that you're receiving from the leadership team; how to get a good work/life balance. Friends in school can be very useful in this way. But they also have another use – a more selfish use. They can really help with your own mental health. Having somebody you enjoy seeing at work tends to encourage you and improve performance in your role (Mann, 2018). Think about it, if you feel isolated at your work, you are not going to enjoy it as much.

I. AM. FUMING.

You've probably already had stressful days as a student-teacher, maybe because there have been behaviour issues; parents phoning with ridiculous complaints or simply that the children still can't understand the concept you're trying to teach. For these, and many more reasons in school, you are likely to be angry, annoyed or upset. As such, it is really important to have a friend that you can go to for a rant.

Have that rant about that child who is causing you extra stress. Yes, we know you don't truly mean it but privately getting that frustration out will only benefit you in the long run (Waines, 2013). Use your time after school to privately rant with your friend. Have a moan about somebody being irritating in your class; rant about the lack of common sense from some children; complain about that lack of organisation from some students. Sometimes, there's a call for having a rant about a decision that the leadership team has made – but, again, keep these minimal and private, you don't want to extend a complaint further than a minor frustration without facing repercussions from the leadership team. Remember, you can also use this time to complain or vent your frustrations about issues at home. Having time to get these stresses out of your system can help you focus and feel better (Seltzer, 2014). These frustrations can potentially lead to tears – and that is okay. In your NQT/Probation year, most people will eventually break down and cry, usually after some really negative feedback; a disastrous lesson or simply the overload of stress and frustrations (Herrera, 2018). I personally do not often show emotion through tears but during my crumbling NQT/Probation year, I received some very harsh feedback for a lesson that I had tried really hard in. I left the meeting, holding things together as best as I possibly could and walked out to the open-plan classrooms to gather resources for the next day. It was here where a colleague asked if I was okay, to which my response was "No," followed by tears. I needed to have my cry (albeit, I wish it wasn't as public as it was) to let out all the stress, anger and emotions that were built up from my stressful year. So, if you need to, have a cry with a colleague and let out all those emotions and frustrations, do it – they'll probably need one too at some point.

Happiness

Teaching is a tough job, and the previous section has probably done nothing to reassure you. But remember that teaching is a happy job too. Being happy in your job is paramount. Consider the school you work at – are you happy there? Do you have colleagues that you like spending time with or have fun with outside of school? If you are not enjoying the school that you are at, then consider finding a different school to move to. Your happiness will impact how well you can teach your class and how well you can develop your skills as a teacher. Consider whether you are happy in your job. I have met many teachers who have openly said that they hate teaching and would quit if they had another career to go into. I occasionally see posts on social media pages from teachers who have decided to quit teaching altogether because they are no longer happy in their job. It does sadden me to see this and I sincerely hope that if you have similar dissatisfactions in your job that you can work through them to see the joys that come from teaching. But try to look for the happy moments in your job. The hilarious moments that will make anybody laugh. Enjoy those moments. Look for those moments which just fill your heart with joy. A moment that always sticks out for me was a boy who couldn't count to ten or recognise and write his numbers. It took the whole year in primary 1, but when he got there, **everybody** was happy and cheering for him. We effectively had a party for this happy moment. Was that complete overkill? Absolutely. But sometimes, you just have to enjoy those little moments. Sometimes, those little moments mean the most to people.

Summary of Key Points

- Find a friend that you trust to have chats with and ask for non-judgmental advice.
- Having a friend at work is likely to improve your happiness at work.
- Vent your frustrations about your class to a friend – get things off your chest.
- If you need to, have a cry. Just let it all out.
- Consider your happiness – are you happy in your school? Are you happy with your **job**?
- Savour the happy and funny moments from class. Share these funny anecdotes with friends and colleagues. Enjoy your time in school.

Tip #10
Continual Professional Development

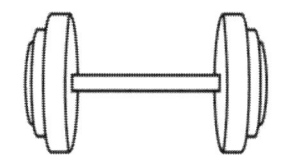

We're Always Learning

As teachers, we are always learning. Furthermore, as teachers, I think we are always wanting to learn. We are always on the lookout for a new resource, skill or training to improve our practice. Unlike most professions, where people go on training courses to allow them to be able to do their job or to make them more employable, teachers tend to go on courses to improve their practice and make them better teachers. Additionally, teachers usually want to fill that 'gap' in their practice that they have been unable to do effectively. Moreover, it's expected as part of your job that you will do CPD as regularly as possible.

However, something that a lot of people forget is that CPD does not have to be an expensive course that lasts 2 hours in your local college or university. It does not have to have some quirky title that you can put on your CV to say that you have done this training or that course. CPD is also what you are doing <u>right now</u> - reading this book to improve your practice. Watching videos on *YouTube* to understand how the 'Water Cycle' works in terms of scientific jargon. Searching on the internet to figure out how to do something which is either part of your teaching practice or part of your administrative tasks. This is all CPD. Anything you do to develop yourself as a practitioner is considered CPD. Currently, I am endeavouring to develop my skills in ICT. Presently, I would consider myself fairly competent with computers. Until you ask about 'coding' or 'programming' – then I panic. I recognise that this is a key component of ICT learning and know that it is something I need to develop to be able to provide the best learning possible for my students. I've had colleagues use apps like *'Duolingo'* or *'Babbel'* to practise their French or German to ensure they felt more confident teaching a foreign language to their class. Please note, I am not stating that you need to spend every waking minute outside of school developing additional skills. But it is worth considering what you think you need to improve on professionally to provide the best education possible at all levels for all learners.

SPECIALISMS

Everybody has their area of expertise. Many teachers use this expertise to become secondary teachers, as they feel more comfortable teaching their subject of choice. However, as primary teachers, we are generally the 'Jack of all Trades, Master of None'. That is in no way belittling your many talents, what I mean is that we, as primary teachers, need to be able to do it all. However, as I mentioned, you may have a secret talent that you can use to your advantage within the school. A colleague of mine was <u>very</u> adept at art and was therefore always able to give her classes art lessons which were <u>above</u> your average teacher's art lesson ability. Further to this, she was usually coerced into painting the backdrops for the school concerts, etc. These little talents don't go unnoticed. SLT generally know who to go to if they need something in particular – and trust me, they will ask for that favour. Where possible, always oblige as it holds you in good stead with them, particularly when you need a favour in return. Another example is from a friend of mine who was very good with computers, knew where all the cables and wires were meant to go and could always do really exciting things within their lessons using technology. The good thing about their specialism was that they were able to recommend some excellent apps to enhance learning; show teachers some shortcuts to save them time with lessons, and help to support some of the more stubborn teachers who were apprehensive to use technology in any capacity (there are still some). The drawback of their talent was that they were the one everybody called for when their computer broke – which was very annoying for them. (Perhaps if you are an ICT specialist, keep it to yourself!)

However, specialisms don't just stop at individual subjects. My specialism is with Early Years children. As a male teacher, this is (arguably) unusual, but a specialism I truly enjoy. I *can* teach further up the school, in fact, I was once tasked with teaching Third Level/KS3 English, History and ICT for a few months in the Secondary School at an International School but I definitely much prefer teaching Early Years. I really enjoy the excitement, the engagement, the noise, and the overall progress that you see in this stage. I spend much of my CPD looking at how I can enhance play-based learning; support the development of reading and writing, and use learning journeys to inspire progression among younger children. Your specialism might be with older students or the middle stages. You may have a particular aptitude for the reading scheme book banding (it's unconventional, but it may be that specialism that the school is looking for). Perhaps you take part in amateur dramatics in your spare time and have the skills to take a school concert from 'Expected' to 'Exceptional'.

A specialism which is usually sought after is in Additional Support Needs. As the majority of schools need to be inclusive of most learning needs, the demand for teachers with specialisms in ASN increases. When I consider the classes I have had in recent years, I have had at least one autistic child (of varying levels) every year for the past five years. Being a specialist in an area of Additional Support Needs is a very rewarding skill to have as it: a) gives you the knowledge and skills to work with a wide range of students; b) gives you the knowledge to support other teachers who are having difficulties with ASN in their class; c) Anything you implement in your class to support a child with any specific ASN will never detrimentally impact the learning of others but instead always enhances it; d) it looks very attractive on a CV. A teacher who has these additional skills or specialisms instantly becomes a lot more valuable to a school who is lacking in these areas.

A colleague of mine discovered that they have a particular aptitude for behaviour management – they just knew how to read all children, including the unpredictable ones. They knew how and when to be firm or nurturing and how to get the best out of these children. Another colleague of mine has become an 'unofficial' autism specialist, purely because she has worked with so many autistic children in her mainstream classes; went on so many courses to support herself in class with autistic children; and, as a result, read so many books on supporting a class with autistic children that she has become quite the expert (even though she claims otherwise!) It may take some time to figure out what your specialism is but don't despair. You don't have to have a specialism by the end of the year – it will come to you over the years.

Master's Degree

Most of my friends and colleagues had this to say when I asked them about the 'Master's in Education' degree: "I've just done four years of essay writing and stress. Why on earth would I want to do another 4-5 years of stress on a part-time basis?!"

I fully understand where they are coming from. Many of you reading this right now may have decided to embark on a Master's Degree while starting your first year of teaching simultaneously. For me, that was not something that interested me. I was more focused on trying to become the best teacher I could be (this, of course, did not go to plan). However, I did begin the Master's in Education two years after my NQT/Probation year, though my friends' and colleagues' sentiments were still very similar: "Why would you want to go back to university? We just got out of there!"

Furthermore, why would you want to do the Master's? In the UK, it often doesn't give you as much compared with other industries. In engineering, a Master's suggests you are more qualified for a position than someone without the Master's. You don't need a Master's qualification in the UK to move into Leadership positions in the primary school, though if you intend on moving into the international circuit, then they do often look for a leadership qualification which can be completed through the Master's Degree.

For me, I discovered that I found 'Education' as a topic very interesting. I genuinely find the research side to be intriguing and I love to find the arguments or 'Devil's Advocate' position in every issue. However, it did mean spending my October and Spring holidays stuck in the library trying to research and write assignments for nearly four years. That was a flaw of the Master's in Education course. However, the positives were the skills that I achieved from it. I consider myself to be able to look at things much more critically than I was able to before; I question happenings or resources more tactfully, and I consider the interpretation of things more analytically.

So, should you do a Master's in Education? There's no easy answer to that. It truly depends on what you want to achieve from it. The Master's expands your theoretical knowledge and critical thinking skills within a school, but it does not necessarily impact directly on your classroom practice by giving you tips or techniques to try. Instead, it tends to indirectly affect your practice. For example, I regularly used the Leuven Scale of Involvement (Laevers, 1994) throughout much of my research during the Master's course to research engagement. This has not fundamentally changed my entire teaching practice, but it has made me consider the notion of engagement in my lessons more. I now think about *who* is engaged; how can I tell; and do I need to adapt my lessons to increase engagement? However, it does take a lot of time and it is a commitment.

You have to consider whether all that work and effort is worth it for a piece of paper that most leadership teams don't require in the UK. Are you doing it for your career, or for you?

Summary of Key Points

- Continual professional development is part of your job. You are always learning as a professional and you should want to develop at all times.
- Consider whether you might have a specialism that you could use at a school. Possibly to lead you into a new career or a new position within the school.
- Consider whether the Master's Degree is the right thing for you. Will it bring you what you want it to bring you, or is it just another four years of stress?

Tip #11

Get A Life

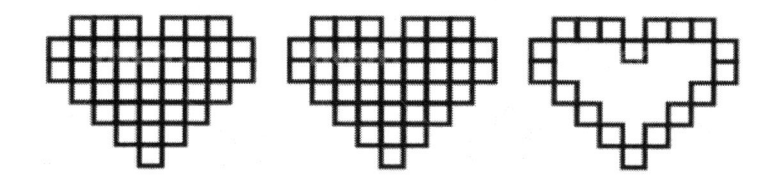

How Long Are You Spending at School?

In my NQT/Probation year, I vividly recall arriving at work at 7am and, often, not leaving the building until after 6:30pm. Then I was going home, having a quick meal and doing more work before going to sleep at 11:00pm. To make matters worse, I often worked on the weekends too. I did this most weeks for the entirety of my first year. This, in no way, had a positive effect on either my practice or my emotional & physical wellbeing. The hours I was putting into my job during the week were far too long.

In your practice, you must maintain a work schedule. More and more teachers are taking more and more of their work home with them (in fact, teachers are not alone in this, many other workers are doing the same). This is not good for you in the long term. It is vitally important that you set time boundaries for yourself: a time when you will **start** and a time when you will **stop**. Right now, for example, I start at 7am and leave work at 4:30pm at the latest. Learning to prioritise your workload will come with time, practise and organisation. By having an end time, it allows you to go home, relax or engage with a social event or hobby. Giving yourself that time where you do no school work is very beneficial. It allows you to have a life outside of school. There will be times where you have to break your schedule and take things home to get them finished. Sometimes, this is unavoidable. Even now after years of teaching, I recognise that some things just need to be done and cannot wait until the morning. You will, with experience, learn what can wait until the next day to be completed and also, over time, gather enough resources that you don't need to spend all evening making them when you could be relaxing instead.

There's a Life Outside of Teaching

Teaching is a very difficult profession. It tears at you emotionally, physically and mentally. I recall being told that teaching was more than just a 'job': it was a vocation. A vocation that you need to be fully dedicated to; something that you need to spend every waking minute and hour improving and thinking about. In your NQT/Probation year, this is probably an accurate depiction (whether you want it to be or not). You will spend a lot of time ensuring you have everything ready for your class; that your marking is completed; your wall displays are perfect. You will probably go home and do more marking; planning; resource making. But when does it all stop?

You must have some form of life outside of school. The classic phrase you will hear is that you need to have a *"Work-Life Balance"*. Usually, in your first year, it's not really an equal balance as you'll tend to do more 'work' than 'life'. During my NQT/Probation year, with my aforementioned insane working hours, I made myself have one afternoon and one evening off per week. Saturday afternoons were when I helped run an amateur sports team: so, between the hours of 10am and 5pm, I was not thinking about school. I also, on occasion, made a point to go out on a Friday or Saturday night to meet friends or family. These were part of my week. Think about what you need: maybe going to the gym; having a date night; meeting with friends; seeing family – something that is for you and lets you focus on something else. You will likely still think about school, even when you are meant to have your mind on other things, but simply having something else to do other than school is important to creating that work-life balance.

Linked to this, consider your holidays. As teachers, we are generally blessed with a multitude of holidays. How are you going to spend your holidays? Are you planning to go away and have time for yourself or are you going to use those days off to catch up with paperwork? It is important to make time for yourself. I should note that some teachers do like to use their holidays to catch up with paperwork; come into school and make those amazing displays, and create their planning for the next few weeks. That is their choice – as experienced teachers, they will know how to manage their work-life balance better. You have to remember that, to some extent, this is still a job – and that you need to still have a life outside of your career.

You

We also have to talk about one of the most important people in the school: you. We need to think about your mental health. All of my previous points regarding your work-life balance are linked to your mental health as a practitioner. As a teacher, stress will usually become part of your life: stress about paperwork; stress about observations; stress about that pupil who misbehaves; stress about the child with additional support needs who is unable to access certain parts of the curriculum. There are several articles which discuss the rise in stress for class teachers (Ferguson, 2019; Brundin, 2020; Herman, Prewitt, et al, 2020) suggesting that it is still very apparent for all teachers – including NQT/Probationer teachers.

In my NQT/Probation year, I definitely suffered from stress. I struggled with a lot of things and they all built up. I didn't talk to anybody about it or explain that I was struggling until it was far too late. Even though it was too late, breaking down and crying in front of colleagues was probably the best thing to happen as I was finally able to open up and talk about the problems I was having. My colleagues could all relate to my difficulties and offer support to me.

If you are struggling, please talk to somebody.

Summary of Key Points

- Consider how long you are spending in the school building – are you spending too long at work?
- Give yourself a schedule: a time you start working and a time you stop working.
- Try to avoid taking things home to do every night. Give yourself a break and try to establish '**Work**' and '**Home**'.
- Have a hobby or regular social event which gives you time away from school and teaching.
- Try to use your holidays as 'Holidays'.
- Look after yourself.
- Speak to someone about how you are feeling.

Tip #12

Expect the Unexpected

Have Something Up Your Sleeve

In teaching, very few things go precisely to plan. When they do, we often relay these lessons to our peers as one of the greatest lessons that we've ever taught. However, more often than not, something will usually affect your perfect lesson: the children don't understand the content; the children are not engaging with the content; the children are bored; the task doesn't match the learners' styles or needs; the task is too easy/hard; the children aren't completing it correctly; the children complete it **very** quickly – the list of things that can affect your lesson is endless. Being adaptable enough to deal with this is vital in your practice but it's also important to have something up your sleeve.

You might have seen many teachers have resources in their classroom for children who finish their task quickly. Often, these 'Fast-Finishers' get the opportunity to do some form of activity which is slightly more relaxing than the task they were previously doing.

This activity changes depending on: the age of the children; the resources available; the subject that they have just finished a task in; and what you, as their teacher, have to offer.

As a class teacher, it is imperative that you have the following things:

- A shared plan of what you expect the children to do when they finish a task.
- Resources available which link to the current task which the children can do to extend or challenge their learning.
- Toys which allow the children to learn.
- A selection of relevant and purposeful tasks which can be used after any lesson.

As mentioned before, the majority of my classroom experience has been with Early Years, which means that most of the activities I had available for the children when they finished a task were play-based. Sometimes, it was giving them free play to allow them to explore and choose what they wanted to learn about or practise. In this instance, it was ensuring that I varied the resources for these children to give them the option in what they wanted to do. I've seen, and used, plenty of Fast-Finisher cards in class, where the children choose an activity card which is linked to Literacy or Maths to allow them to practise a skill. I've used a reading corner, giving the class a range of books to match their interests and a comfy area for them to read. My favourite task for 'Fast-Finishers' was the use of technology. One school I worked in had several sets of tablets and laptops available, which could be used at any time. For many of the children, they loved getting onto technology and this worked as an incentive for children to apply themselves to their learning. In particular, I enjoyed using apps such as Sumdog©, for maths, and Duolingo©, for teaching the children a language (this one, in particular, was very useful for the older children and showed progression throughout the year). Consider what resources you have but also what you want your learners to achieve once they've finished the original task that you set for them.

The majority of these 'Fast-Finishers' occur when there are only 10-15 minutes left of the lesson and you simply need something to keep them learning for the remainder of the lesson while you support the rest of the class to achieve their learning goals. But what about when **everyone** has finished the task after only 15 minutes. I recall this happening in my second year out of NQT/Probation. I had spent two and a half hours cutting hundreds of little squares and laminating them so that I could reuse them in the future for this incredible discussion and matching lesson I had planned for my topic on children's toys. This was going to be the lesson that put my face on the map of teaching. The lesson that people from other schools talked about being ground-breaking.

The entire class finished the lesson and were bored of it after 6 minutes. What on earth was I going to do for the remaining 54 minutes of the school day?!

This, for me, was a key learning experience in my practice: always have a bank of back-up lessons that you can use at **any** time. Lessons, that you can use at any given moment to productively fill in a gap in your timetable. Try to have a selection of lessons which will suit younger children and a different set that can suit older children.

Sometimes, you might need these lessons for other reasons. The specialist teacher might be absent on the day you have them and you have to cover that lesson. Sometimes this is fine, and you can follow the specialist's plan or make up something relevant to the subject (I think about things like P.E. where there is always a sport you can play with them). But what about the specialist classes that you might not know how to cover, such as foreign languages? You might even be asked to cover a colleague's class for an hour while they have a meeting. Again, usually, they would let you know what the lesson is and you can simply give the lesson as best as you can. Other times, you might have to improvise. It's vital to have a bank of these lessons which can fill any gaps in the timetable at the last minute, especially ones which require minimal planning or resources for you.

How On Earth Did That Happen?

I truly love teaching. It's one of the best decisions I ever made. There are so many amazing benefits to being a teacher. Seeing children reach their full potential; helping a child overcome that challenge that has plagued them; being that person that the child trusts with their life is truly a privilege. Going from being just another person in the community to a celebrity and a key person in the lives of both the children and their parents is truly remarkable.

Sometimes, however, strange things happen in your class. Children can get into the most ridiculous of situations and even say the most random things. First, make sure, no matter what the scenario or conversation is, that everyone is safe. That is key. Then deal with the scenario.

In this instance, I am unable to share much more advice than this, as there is no way of preparing you for the randomness that is school and what could happen. I've seen children getting their head stuck between railings; children losing their clothes (to this day I still don't know how); children swallowing glue and children asking the most bizarre questions. At the time, you will experience sheer panic, but afterwards, you'll have a great anecdote for the staffroom and your friends.

Summary of Key Points

- Have a plan of action for children who finish lessons quickly – but ensure they are worthwhile activities.
- Have a set of back up lessons which can be applied to any scenario.
- Expect the unexpected. Schools are places filled with random experiences – ensure safety first and then enjoy the hilarity and ridiculousness.

A Final Word

To close, I sincerely hope that this book has given you some practical and honest advice. Whether this is your NQT/Probation year or if you've been teaching for many years, I wish you the best of luck in all your endeavours in teaching. It truly is the most rewarding job in the world.

References

AGGOR, N., 2014. *HOW TO MAKE SUCCESSFUL STUDENTS IN ONE YEAR - A MODEL FOR THE WORLD.* Bloomington, IN: AuthorHouse LLC.

BRUNDIN, J., 2020. *When Teachers Are Stressed, Students Are Stressed. This Program Is Trying To Help Teachers Cope.* [Online]
Available at: https://www.cpr.org/2020/02/11/when-teachers-are-stressed-students-are-stressed-this-program-is-trying-to-help-teachers-cope/
[Accessed 19 October 2020].

BRUNER, J. S., 1960. *The Process of Education.* Cambridge, MA: Harvard University Press.

BRYCE-CLEGG, A., 2015. *Best Practice in the Early Years.* London: Bloomsbury.

BUSBY, E., 2019. *Parents should be stopped from withdrawing children from religious education over Islam lessons, headteachers say.* [Online]
Available at:
https://www.independent.co.uk/news/education/education-news/parents-religious-education-islam-headteachers-liverpool-hope-university-study-a8976366.html
[Accessed 20 October 2020].

CANADIAN CENTRE FOR CHILD PROTECTION INC, 2018. The Prevalence of Sexual Abuse by K-12 School Personnel in Canada, 1997–2017. *Journal of Child Sexual Abuse,* 28(1), pp. 46-66.

CARLSON, T., 2020. *Yes, I Hug My Students. Research Says You Should Too.* [Online]
Available at: https://www.edsurge.com/news/2020-02-07-yes-i-hug-my-students-research-says-you-should-too
[Accessed 15 May 2020].

CHAPLAIN, R., 2015. Rules, Routines and Rituals in Behaviour Management. In: M. Gregson, L. Nixon, A. Pollard & T. Spedding, eds.

Readings for Reflective Teaching in Further, Adult and Vocational Education. London: Bloomsbury Academic, pp. 106-109.

CHESEBROUGH, E. & KING, P., 2004. Bingham Early Childhood Prosocial Curriculum. In: E. Chesebrough, P. King, M. Bloom & T. P. Gullotta, eds. *A Blueprint for the Promotion of Pro-Social Behavior in Early Childhood.* New York, NY: Kluwer Academic/Plenum Publishers, pp. 155-390.

COELHO, E., 2012. *Language and Learning in Multilingual Classrooms: A Practical Approach.* Bristol: Multlingual Matters.

COHEN, L., MANION, L. & MORRISON, K., 2004. *A Guide to Teaching Practice.* 5th ed. London: Routledge.

CONKIN, W., 2010. *Applying Differentiation Strategies: Grades K-2.* 2nd ed. Huntington Beach, CA: Shell Education.

COX, R. D. & SCHOPLER, E., 1993. Aggression and self-injurious behaviors in persons with autism: The TEACCH approach. *Acta Paedopsychiatrica: International Journal of Child & Adolescent Psychiatry,* 56(2), pp. 85-90.

CRUICKSHANK, V., 2018. Male primary teachers' fear and uncertainty surrounding physical contact. *Education 3-13,* 47(2), pp. 247-257.

CUSHMAN, P., 2005. Let's hear it from the males: Issues facing male primary school teachers. *Teaching and Teacher Education: An International Journal of Research and Studies,* 21(3), pp. 227-240.

DEPARTMENT FOR EDUCATION, 2013. *National Curriculum in England,* London: Department for Education.

DIAZ, C., 2019. *Understanding the 8 Types Of Learning Styles.* [Online] Available at: https://blog.mindvalley.com/types-of-learning-styles/ [Accessed 13 May 2020].

DODD, J. L., 2012. *Augmentative and Alternative Communication Intervention: An Intensive, Immersive, Socially-based Service Delivery Model.* San Diego, CA: Plural Publishing, Inc..

DUNN, D., 2017. *How to Be an Outstanding Primary School Teacher.* 2nd ed. London: Bloomsbury Education.

ELLIOT, S. N., KRATOCHWILL, T. R., LITTLEFIELD COOK, J. & TRAVERS, J., 2000. *Educational psychology: Effective teaching, effective learning.* 3rd ed. Boston, MA: McGraw-Hill College.

FERGUSON, D., 2019. *Record levels of stress 'put teachers at breaking point'.* [Online]
Available at: https://www.theguardian.com/education/2019/nov/10/stressed-teachers-at-breaking-point-says-report
[Accessed 3 October 2020].

FROMBERG, D. P., 2012. *The All-Day Kindergarten and Pre-K Curriculum: A Dynamic-Themes Approach.* Abingdon: Routledge.

GARDNER, H., 1983. *Frames of mind: The theory of multiple intelligences.* New York, NY: Basic Books.

GERSHON, M., 2018. *How to Use Bloom's Taxonomy in the Classroom The Complete Guide.* West Palm Beach, FL: Learning Sciences International.

GRANT, R., 2019. *'Grouping primary children by ability is indefensible'.* [Online]
Available at: https://www.tes.com/news/grouping-primary-children-ability-indefensible
[Accessed 1 May 2020].

HARGREAVES, A. & FULLAN, M., 2012. *Professional Capital: Transformng Teaching in Every School.* New York, NY: Teachers College Press.

HARGREAVES, E., 2017. *Children's Experiences of Classrooms: Talking about Being Pupils in the Classroom.* London: SAGE Publications Ltd.

HATTIE, J., 2008. *Visible Learning: A Synthesis of Over 800 Meta-Analyses Relating to Achievement.* Abingdon: Routledge.

HATTIE, J., 2012. *Visible Learning for Teachers: Maximizing Impact on Learning.* Abingdon: Routledge.

HERMAN, K. C. et al., 2020. Profiles of middle school teacher stress and coping: Concurrent and prospective correlates. *Journal of School Psychology,* Volume 78, pp. 54-68.

HERRERA, T., 2018. *Why You Shouldn't Feel Bad About Crying at Work: When was the last time you had a good work cry?.* [Online]
Available at: https://www.nytimes.com/2018/10/14/smarter-living/crying-at-work.html
[Accessed 14 November 2020].

HUDSON, H., 2019. *Can I Hug My Students? Teachers Weigh In.* [Online]
Available at: https://www.weareteachers.com/can-i-hug-my-students/
[Accessed 14 May 2020].

JACKSON, A. W., 2004. *Making the Most of Middle School: A Field Guide for Parents and Others.* New York, NY: Teachers College Press.

JOHNSON, C. A., 2019. *Go ahead and look up your kid's teacher on social media — just tread carefully.* [Online]
Available at: https://www.chicagotribune.com/lifestyles/sc-fam-social-graces-teacher-on-social-media-0820-20190823-56z7kfidfbhmfbvkydknxijx7m-story.html
[Accessed 15 May 2020].

JONES, D., 2009. Constructing Identities: perceptions and experiences of male head teachers. In: D. Jones & R. Evans, eds. *Men in the Lives of Young Children: An international perspective.* Abingdon: Routledge, pp. 30-43.

KATZ, L. G., CHARD, S. C. & KOGAN, Y., 2014. *Engaging Children's Minds: The Project Approach.* 3rd ed. Santa Barbara, CA: ABC-CLIO, LLC.

KNOESTER, M., 2012. *Democratic Education in Practice: Inside the Mission Hill School.* New York, NY: Teachers College Press.

KOLB, D. A., 1984. *Experiential learning: Experience as the source of learning and development (Vol. 1).* 1st ed. Englewood Cliffs, NJ: Prentice-Hall.

KRESS, G. et al., 2005. *English in Urban Classrooms: A Multimodal Perspective on Teaching and Learning.* Abingdon: RoutledgeFalmer.

LAEVERS, F., 1994. *The Leuven Involvement Scale for Young Children LIS-YC.* Leuven: Centre for Experimental Education.

LINSIN, M., 2009. *Dream Class: How To Transform Any Group Of Students Into The Class You've Always Wanted.* San Diego, CA: JME Publishing.

LINSIN, M., 2013. *The Classroom Management Secret: And 45 Other Keys to a Well-Behaved Class.* San Diego, CA: JME Publishing.

LINSIN, M., 2014. *Classroom Management for Art, Music, and PE Teachers.* San Diego, CA: JME Publishing.

LOEWENBERG, A., 2017. *There's a Stigma Around Men Teaching Young Kids. Here's How We Change It.* [Online]
Available at: https://slate.com/human-interest/2017/10/a-male-preschool-teacher-reflects-on-the-stigma-keeping-men-out-of-pre-k-classrooms.html
[Accessed 17 May 2020].

LOVEWELL, K., 2012. *Every Teacher Matters.* St Albans: Ecademy Press.

MACKINNON, B. & FIALA, A., 2018. *Ethics: Theory and Contemporary Issues.* 9th ed. Boston, MA: Cengage Learning.

MADEJ, K., 2016. *Physical Play and Children's Digital Games.* Cham: Springer.

MANN, A., 2018. *Why We Need Best Friends At Work.* [Online]
Available at: https://www.gallup.com/workplace/236213/why-need-best-friends-work.aspx
[Accessed 14 November 2020].

McEWAN, E. K., 2006. *How to Survive and Thrive in the First Three Weeks of School.* Thousand Oaks, CA: Corwin Press.

MEAD, L., 2017. Importance of Play-Based Learning in Early Childhood. In: G. Geng, P. Smith & P. Black, eds. *The Challenge of Teaching: Through the Eyes of Pre-service Teachers.* Singapore: Springer, pp. 115-122.

MILLER, D. F., 2016. *Positive Child Guidance.* 8th ed. Boston, MA: Cengage Learning.

NATIONAL LITERACY TRUST, 2017. *Adult literacy: Information on adult literacy in the UK and our Books Unlocked programme.* [Online]
Available at: https://literacytrust.org.uk/parents-and-families/adult-

literacy/#:~:text=1%20in%206%20(16.4%25%20%2F,have%20very%20poor%20literacy%20skills.
[Accessed 15 November 2020].

NICKELSEN, L., 2001. *Teaching Elaboration and Word Choice.* New York, NY: Scholastic Inc.

OPTIZ, M. F., 1998. *Flexible Grouping in Reading: Practical Ways to Help All Students Become Stronger Readers.* New York, NY: Scholastic Inc.

PIAGET, J., 1936. *Origins of intelligence in the child.* 1st ed. London: Routledge & Kegan Paul.

PLEVIN, R., 2016. *Take Control of the Noisy Class: Chaos to Calm in 15 Seconds.* s.l.:Life Raft Media Ltd.

PLEVIN, R., 2017. *Classroom Management Success in 7 Days or Less: The Ultra-Effective Classroom Management System for Teachers.* s.l.:Life Raft Media Ltd.

RADFORD, L., 2012. *Rethinking Children, Violence and Safeguarding.* London: Continuum International Publishing Group.

REINKE, W. M., HERMAN, K. C. & SPRICK, R., 2011. *Motivational Interviewing for Effective Classroom Management: The Classroom Check-Up.* New York, NY: The Guilford Press.

REIST, M., 2011. *Raising Boys in a New Kind of World.* Lancaster: Gazelle Book Services Limited.

ROSE, R. & HOWLEY, M., 2007. *The Practical Guide to Special Educational Needs in Inclusive Primary Classrooms.* Paul Chapman Publishing: London.

ŞALLI-ÇOPUR, D., 2005. Coping with the Problems of Mixed Ability Classes. *The Internet TESL Journal,* 11(8).

SCHLECHTY, P. C., 2011. *Engaging Students: The Next Level of Working on the Work.* San Francisco, CA: Josey-Bass.

SCHOPLER, E., 1994. Behavioral priorities for autism and related developmental disorders. In: E. Schopler & G. B. Mesibov, eds. *Behavioral issues in autism.* New York, NY: Plenham Press, pp. 55-75.

SCOTTISH EXECUTIVE, 2004. *A Curriculum for Excellence,* Edinburgh: Scottish Executive.

SCOTTISH GOVERNMENT, 2009. *Curriculum for Excellence - Building the Curriculum 4: Skills for Learning, Skills for Life and Skills for Work,* Edinburgh: Scottish Government.

SCOTTISH GOVERNMENT, 2019. *Pupil Census Supplementary Data, 2018.* [Online]
Available at: https://www2.gov.scot/Topics/Statistics/Browse/School-Education/dspupcensus
[Accessed 26 April 2020].

SELTZER, L. F., 2014. *6 Virtues, and 6 Vices, of Venting.* [Online]
Available at: https://www.psychologytoday.com/us/blog/evolution-the-self/201404/6-virtues-and-6-vices-venting#:~:text=Generally%2C%20it's%20better%20to%20let,indignity%2C%20misfortune%2C%20or%20injustice.
[Accessed 14 November 2020].

SILVERMAN, P. R., 2004. *Widow to Widow: How the Bereaved Help One Another.* 2nd ed. Hove: Brunner-Routledge.

SLAVIN, R. E., MADDEN, N. A., CHAMBERS, B. & HAXBY, B., 2009. *2 Million Children: Success for All.* 2nd ed. London: SAGE Ltd.

SMALLEY, P., 2018. *Parents are pulling children from RE lessons – so they don't learn about Islam.* [Online]
Available at: https://theconversation.com/parents-are-pulling-children-from-re-lessons-so-they-dont-learn-about-islam-95235
[Accessed 20 October 2020].

SNOW, K., 2017. *Addition Facts that Stick: Help Your Child Master the Addition Facts for Good in Just Six Weeks (Facts That Stick).* Charles City, VA: Well-Trained Mind Press.

SOUSA, D. A., 2009. *How the Brain Influences Behavior: Management Strategies for Every Classroom.* Thousand Oaks, CA: Corwin Press.

TAFFEL, R., 2012. *The Decline And Fall Of Parental Authority and What Therapists Can Do About It.* [Online]

Available at: https://www.psychotherapynetworker.org/magazine/article/287/the-decline-and-fall-of-parental-authority [Accessed 15 November 2020].

TOMLINSON, C. A. & ALLAN, S. D., 2000. *Leadership for Differentiating Schools & Classrooms.* Alexandria, VA: ASCD.

VYGOTSKY, L., 1978. *Mind in society: The development of higher psychological processes.* 1st ed. Cambridge, MA: Harvard University Press.

WAINES, A., 2013. *The Self-Esteem Journal.* 2nd ed. London: Sheldon Press.

WENDLING, K., 2007. Education in a Liberal Society: Implications of Ross. In: S. Brennan & R. Noggle, eds. *Taking Responsibility for Children.* Waterloo, Ontario: Wilfrid Laurier University Press, pp. 139-156.

WHITE, J., 2019. *Playing and Learning Outdoors: The Practical Guide and Sourcebook for Excellence in Outdoor Provision and Practice with Young Children.* 3rd ed. Abingdon: Routledge.

WILLIAMS, L., 2017. *Positive Behaviour Management in Early Years Settings: An Essential Guide.* London: Jessica Kingsley Publishers.

WILLIAMS, L., 2018. *Positive Behaviour Management in Primary Schools: An Essential Guide.* London: Jessica Kingsley Publishers.

WILLIAMSON, J., 2008. *Literacy in the Student-Centered Classroom: A Practical Approach to Setup, Design, and Implementation.* Plymouth: Rowman & Littlefield Education.

WINOGRAD, K., 2009. An Exploratory Study of Race and Religion in the Emotional Experience of African-American Female Teachers. In: P. A. Schutz & M. Zembylas, eds. *Advances in Teacher Emotion Research: The Impact on Teachers' Lives.* London: Springer, pp. 299-322.

WRAGG, E. C., 1993. *Primary Teaching Skills.* 1st ed. London: Routledge.

Index

A

additional support needs · 10, 42, 112
Additional Support Needs · 104
aggressive · 42, 65
area · 4, 5, 6, 9, 14, 17, 23, 28, 34, 43, 66, 67, 78, 85, 88, 104, 115
assessments · 19, 35

B

baseline assessments · 19
behaviour · 9, 27, 28, 29, 31, 40, 41, 42, 46, 65, 72, 88, 91, 97, 104
Bloom's Taxonomy · 57

C

care · 17, 43, 60, 61, 66, 72, 107
Child protection · 17
Child Protection · 43, 60, 67
Children · 23, 41, 42, 53, 63, 117
Chronology · 67
classroom · 2, 6, 7, 8, 12, 16, 19, 20, 23, 24, 26, 27, 28, 29, 30, 31, 34, 40, 43, 44, 50, 53, 55, 62, 66, 70, 75, 91, 93, 106, 114
classroom management · 19, 24, 26, 28, 32, 44, 93
classroom management plan · 19, 93
Classroom Setup · 6, 9, 12, 16
Cognitivism · 57
colleagues · 8, 65, 77, 79, 81, 85, 92, 98, 100, 102, 105
commitment · 42, 77, 78, 81, 106
community · 4, 5, 6, 20, 63, 78, 117
Constructivism · 52, 57
councils · 73
CPD · 101, 103
Curricular · *See* Curriculum
Curriculum · 13, 14, 15, 57

D

Differentiation · 53
display · *See* Displays
Displays · 9, 10

E

EAL · 11
Early Years · 23, 25, 103, 115
education · 44, 71, 74, 76, 88, 89, 102
emotional neglect · 61
Experiential Learning Cycle · 58

F

families · 6, 67
family · 30, 43, 45, 67, 69, 78, 111
Fast-Finishers · 114, 115, 116
first day · 21, 40, 47
flexible groupings · *See* grouping
Fluid grouping · *See* grouping
friend · 27, 96, 97, 100, 103
frustrations · 97, 100

G

Gardner · 55, 57

groupings · 33, 34, 35, 40, 54

H

handover notes · 10, 41
happiness · 98, 100
homework · 23, 30, 40, 90, 95

I

illiteracy · 90

L

learners · 14, 35, 49, 54, 56, 57, 69, 70, 75, 102, 114, 116
learning · 5, 6, 9, 10, 12, 14, 16, 18, 30, 33, 34, 35, 36, 37, 40, 42, 44, 47, 50, 52, 53, 54, 55, 56, 57, 59, 62, 66, 85, 90, 93, 101, 102, 103, 108, 115, 116
Learning Assistant · 90
Learning Journeys · 9
learning styles · 55, 57
lessons · 19, 36, 40, 44, 48, 49, 50, 51, 54, 57, 59, 71, 74, 96, 102, 106, 114, 116, 117, 119

M

Master's · 105
Masters Degree · 105, 106, 108
medical · 42, 43
mentor · 19, 55, 59, 75, 79, 81
Mixed-Ability Grouping' · *See* grouping

N

neglect · 43, 66
Neglect: Emotional Neglect · 61

O

organisation · 97, 109
Outdoor Learning · 56

P

paperwork · 38, 50, 75, 76, 111, 112
Parent Council · 78
Parental involvement · 88
parents · 4, 5, 22, 43, 49, 66, 68, 69, 71, 79, 82, 84, 87, 88, 89, 91, 92, 93, 95, 97, 117
Parents · 71, 87, 88, 89, 92
personal views · 69
physical contact · 61, 72
Planning · 36
play-based · 56, 103, 115
plenary · 52, 53
political · 69, 72, 82
Primary 1 · 23, 27, 30, 31
probation · 97, 109, 110, 112, 116
probationer · 74, 75, 76, 78, 112
professionalism · 77, 84, 86, 87

R

Reception · 23, 27, 30, 31
relationship · 43, 44, 45, 72, 83, 88, 89
religion · *See* religious
religious · 69, 70, 72
Resources · 12, 115
routines · 19, 23, 27, 40, 71

S

Safety · 60, 62, 63, 66, 69
Scotland · 2, 11, 37, 51
Senior Leadership Team · 6, 76, 84
short-term plans · 36
Social Media · 82
Social Work · 68
specialisms · *See* specialist

specialist · 48, 103, 104, 117
staff · 5, 6, 16, 19, 20, 61, 62, 85
stress · 10, 85, 98, 105, 108, 112
support · 5, 10, 11, 12, 16, 18, 30, 33, 34, 35, 36, 40, 42, 43, 54, 55, 57, 59, 68, 75, 76, 78, 81, 83, 88, 89, 91, 95, 103, 104, 105, 112, 116
systems · 16, 17, 20

T

teacher training · 2, 5, 6, 16, 33, 36, 52, 79
teaching · 1, 3, 5, 6, 8, 12, 14, 16, 19, 20, 22, 25, 26, 28, 29, 30, 31, 36, 38, 42, 45, 50, 51, 56, 57, 59, 60, 62, 67, 69, 70, 72, 74, 78, 79, 84, 85, 89, 91, 98, 102, 103, 106, 110, 113, 114, 116, 117

Technology · 62
timetable · 19, 48, 49, 59, 116, 117

V

violent · 63, 65, 72
Vygotsky · 55, 57

W

wellbeing · 61, 109
work-life balance · 111
Work-Life Balance · 110

Z

Zone of Proximal Development · 57

Printed in Great Britain
by Amazon